To Pam Parker

THE STOKES TWINS RIDE
THE OKLAHOMA WILDCAT

World War II-European Theater

By

Madlyn V. Stokes

_May God bless your
reading of our book
Madlyn V. Stokes
Claude H Stokes
Wph Stern_

Booksurge.com/GreatUNpublished

BOOKSURGE
5341 Dorchester Road
North Charleston, South Carolina
Copyright 2003 by Madlyn V. Stokes
Library of Congress Cataloging – Pending
ISBN 1-58898-839-2

DEDICATION

In loving memory of Jess Whitmore and Nancy Stokes,

For Claude and Clyde,

Family members of the

636th Tank Destroyer Battalion, and

The 36th Infantry Division

ACKNOWLEDGEMENTS

Thanks to my mentor Sharon Ervin for encouragement and guidance as she gave me confidence in reaching my potential, for Connie Kiesewetter who led the McSherry Writers Guild in critiquing my work, and for Priscilla Maine for advising me.

Thanks to Francis and Billie Stipe who inspired me to begin my manuscript with their gift of a computer system, and for our daughter, Lana who suggested the title.

Special thanks to Diana Alles for her expert assistance with the computer, and her daughter, Victoria Alles for her expertise in scanning photos.

To Lorna Pool for copying, our grandson, Brent Harris for long distance phone calls to help me out of computer jams, our grandson, Chad Harris and wife, Daria, for critiquing, encouragement of Vern, Kay, and Tiffani Harris, and for Tyler McBee as he gave advice in styling the manuscript.

Further thanks to Bill Capshaw and son for taking time to look for the Oklahoma Wildcat M 10 tank, and to all of our many friends, who prayed for my writing; especially, Norene Humphries, Wilma Adams, Lynelle Emmons, Jo Kellogg, Earl and Alma Dunn.

Finally, my heartfelt thanks to, Susie Hass and Sabrina Johnson who completed the formatting in readiness for publishing.

May God's blessings be with each of you.

TABLE OF CONTENTS

PROLOGUE

"Here we go again men! Looks like our infantry is going to take a beating on this river crossing," Claude exclaimed.

"We'll be lucky if we come out of this one alive."

In January of 1944, the Stokes twins were attempting to cross the Rapedo River in the Oklahoma Wildcat M10 tank as they supported the 36th Division. They had to cross this same river many times as it wound through the mountains but this encounter with the German tanks and infantry was to be the most costly in the loss of lives.

Claude explained the fierce battle. "The Germans had every inch covered with heavy mortar, machine guns, artillery fire, and what we called the Screaming Memie gun which had a six barrel mortar called Nebwerfer.

"Old Screaming Memie had the grinding roar somewhat like a huge motor having difficulty starting, combined with the sound of hundreds of large-winged birds fluttering right overhead. That loud whirling screech would scare the pants right off anyone in its pathway.

"No one was exempted from danger of the German firepower as we crossed the river. At this particular point of crossing, it probably measured one hundred feet across. We, as well as the Germans, were dug in and returning fire across the river.

"Clyde was driving the Oklahoma Wildcat like a seasoned pro, which he surely was. Cpl. Daniel Sklar, the gunner, was pouring on the shots as directed, and I might add, with great skill. We fired our

3/50mm gun so long and fast that the barrel got so hot it would not go back into recoil preventing it from firing.

"As commander of the Oklahoma Wildcat, I waited until the German firepower slowed down and took a bucket, ran to the river, and carried water to cool off the gun barrel.

"On one of the trips, I didn't make it back to the tank before the shelling started again. I jumped into the slit trench I had dug just for this kind of emergency. As I lay face down for protection, I heard a frying, sizzling sound in the mud nearby. I turned my head and saw the nose of an 8-inch artillery shell sticking in the muddy bank of my slit trench about six inches from my head.

"I reasoned, since the shell did not explode on impact, I had about fifteen seconds to make a most important decision. I could jump out of the trench, which would give me a 95% chance of getting wounded or killed by steel fragments from the shell or machine gun fire from the enemy. If I stayed in the trench, I could take my chance on the shell being a dud.

"The seconds were ticking away. Which decision would I make?"…

Many questions could be asked about the miracles of life and death…

Why did Claude and Clyde live through that terrible battle when 1600 men of the 36th Division were wounded or killed that night? Why was a truce called to pick up the dead and wounded of both American and German soldiers as they lay in a blood-filled river?

Why did Claude and Clyde escape death so many times on the farm and during World War II? How and why did they survive with eight others out of one hundred twenty-eight original men in C Company of the 636th Tank Destroyer Battalion?

The answer to those questions and others one might ask can be answered by beginning at their birth to the present day. The secrets of their success in life can be gleaned from the pages of this book.

INTRODUCTION

The story of the Stokes twins, Claude H. and Clyde T. from McAlester, Oklahoma, who rode the 'Oklahoma Wildcat' M10 tank is long overdue. They served in the United States Army, 636th Tank Destroyer Battalion, supporting, the 36th Division, in World War II. They received the Silver and Bronze Stars for gallantry in action, while serving through five major campaigns in the European Theater of War, from September 9, 1943, to March 11, 1945.

Clyde and Claude

The Stokes twins served together because of a letter, signed by President Franklin D. Roosevelt, ordering that they never be separated as long as they served in the military. (Picture to the right)

Many times over the last fifty-five years Claude and Clyde received letters and telephone calls of inquiry concerning their experiences in World War II with the Oklahoma Wildcat. They received requests from the families of loved ones who had given their lives on the battlefield while serving our great country. Additional inquiries came from movie producers, authors of books, and history teachers in schools and universities. Others came from history buffs and great Americans, interested in experiences of the Stokes twins as they commanded and drove the Oklahoma Wildcat through miraculous escapes in combat, introduced to them in articles appearing across our nation, in England, and other parts of our world.[1] Perhaps, through this book, we can bring some joy, peace, and closure to those who sought information, whether it was for personal comfort or historical interest.

As inquiries came to Claude and Clyde, life was very busy for them as they worked diligently to make a place for themselves as good citizens and providing for their families. Upon retirement from their secular jobs, requests became more frequent for them to appear before history classes and give students their experiences. Teachers were overwhelmed to learn of facts they had never heard concerning the history they had been teaching.

Clyde and Claude
Letter from England, ASSOC Press

'Old soldiers never die, they just fade away' is a cliché that has been repeated many times. Having known Claude and Clyde for the past fifty-nine years, and having been married to Claude for fifty-five years, made me the logical one to write first-hand accounts of their harrowing, and sometimes humorous stories, repeatedly, from tank battles in World War II. Throughout the years valuable artifacts were collected about their adventures, although we never dreamed of writing a book. As we became aware of all the documented material in our possession, I felt compelled to write their story.

Minimal research was required as Claude and Clyde had all their newspaper clippings, scrapbooks we had kept for them, plus many pictures, and a collection of 36th Division history books. We were amazed to find in our possession a wealth of history in one newspaper, *The Oklahoma City Times*, dated May 7, 1945, relating the end of the war with Germany and detailing the war back to 1939. Apparently, God had placed this material in our hands to encourage veterans who were unable to talk about their war experiences, and to inspire our nation of young people to hold on to the great heritage that had been left to them. Someday these two brave soldiers will go to be with God, but through this book, may their memory never fade away.

On July 2, 2000, at The First Baptist Church, of McAlester, Oklahoma, our church family was privileged to hear Claude speak. His Independence Day speech was so moving, I knew I must get my priorities in order and write this book. Time was slipping away for *The Greatest Generation.*

His speech that evening was very heart-warming. He began his speech by saying, "For two hundred and twenty four years we have been blessed as a nation. On July 4, 1776, the Continental Congress declared July 4th a legal holiday. All good things come with a price. Of that price I am here to remind you.

"On December 7, 1941, Japan bombed Pearl Harbor, plunging the United States into World War II. As a soldier in that war, I am here to give you my personal involvement and some first-hand accounts of young men, whom I witnessed, giving their lives that you and I might have the freedom we enjoy today."

After speaking twenty minutes, Claude concluded with this story, "We were fighting a fierce battle in Italy. The Oklahoma Wildcat had been sent in for repairs, resulting in our having to fight with a replacement M10 tank. During this intense battle, the Germans knocked out our second tank, with Clyde and I barely escaping.

"We continued on foot with our infantry, attempting to fight our way out of the great peril in which we found ourselves. We were dodging mortar, going in and out of a wooded area we had previously taken, when we came upon one of our mortar crews of six men. I glanced around and thought all six had been killed. I turned to walk away when I heard a young man crying. As I looked closer I found what I considered a young replacement soldier who had just been sent to the front lines. Just a kid, I thought, because of his clean-shaven face and his clean clothes. The men who had died beside him had beards and wore dirty clothing. The young man was probably no older than Clyde and me. We just felt older and were considered old mature soldiers because we had been fighting for approximately six months. As I looked at this young soldier, so fresh on the battlefield, I knew there was no need to call the medics, as his wounds could not be helped. I cradled his head in my arms and the last words he spoke as he lay dying were, 'I want my Mother.' "

Needless to say, tears from the congregation were being wiped away. It was evident that Claude's words sank deeply into our hearts causing us to pledge ourselves to become better citizens of this beloved nation. The time had come to write the book about their life-long adventures.

Claude and Clyde still look alike and are often mistaken for each other in public. Probably, there are not any twins that are exactly alike. Their differences make a wonderful relationship between them. God gifted them with individual personalities, thus creating ideal teammates to carry on the varied tasks He has called them to do.

Claude is an extrovert with a sanguine personality. He is a born leader, loves to tell stories and has such a humorous way of telling accounts that captivates his audience. Those who hear his vivid episodes find them most interesting, descriptive, and colored with humor.

Clyde is an introvert and has a melancholy personality. He is the quiet one in manner and allows Claude to do most of the talking. He is most patient with Claude, and allows him to be the main spokesman, with his good humor accounts of their tales as they grew up on the farm and battled their way through the bloody campaigns in Europe. Clyde does, at times with his gentle manner, add additional facts to Claude's stories.

Clyde and Claude

In reading this book, one might notice Claude's name more often than Clydes', however he is an equal to Claude. They still reside in McAlester, Oklahoma, are members of the same First Baptist Church, and go to the same Busy Bee Coffee Shop each morning. They even drive automobiles alike. Their blue Buick La Sabres were purchased at the same time. Their loyalty and love for each other is above reproach.

In times of war most tanks were given names by the men who were in command of the individual tanks. The tanks were usually named after girl friends, wives, or movie stars, but the Stokes twins changed the name of their M 10 tank from 'Jinx' to the 'Oklahoma

Wildcat'. This well-known tank remained with the twins throughout their serving together for nineteen months in the European Theater of World War II.

Imagine the excitement of the brothers, in October 2000, as Claude was

Oklahoma Wildcat

talking to one of his old tank buddies, Tom Holcomb, Mount Pleasant, Texas. He related of his seeing the old Oklahoma Wildcat in Texarkana, Texas, near the Red River Ammunition Depot. Investigation is under way at this time to locate and reunite the Oklahoma Wildcat with the Stokes twins.

Statistics reveal that more than 1,200 World War II veterans are passing from the scene each day. It is alarming that we will no longer have access to the first-hand experiences of *The Greatest Generation.*

Our prayer is that through the lives of these brothers and their narrow escapes from death, each of us may realize we have a purpose to fulfill in our lives through God's leadership.

May we never forget the sacrifice and courage that thousands of Americans have made to protect and insure our freedom, not only in World War II, but all veterans who served in our Armed Forces, and will continue to protect our nation in the future. May we always be recognized as *One Nation, Under God.*

"Oh, give thanks unto the Lord; for He is good: for His mercy endureth forever." Psalm 118: 29 (King James Version)

-1-

Early Years Of The Stokes Twins

Jess Whitmore Stokes and Nancy Jane Bagley were married on April 13, 1914, in Dierks, Arkansas.   They were blessed with nine children; however, only five lived. The children born to this union were as follows: Carl Emmit born April 22, 1915; Baby Stokes born and died at birth in July, 1917, Harvey born on December 17, 1919 and died in November, 1922, La Vern Stokes Aldridge born June 28, 1921, twins, Claude and Clyde; born November 17, 1923, Baby Stokes born, and died July 15, 1925, Jesse Lee born February 21,1930 and died June 1931, and Eupal Lee Stokes Harmon born March 2, 1934.

* * *

"No man is poor who has had a Godly mother."

(Abraham Lincoln)

"I'm sorry Mrs. Stokes but I am going to confine you to bed for the last two months of your pregnancy," a Dierks, Arkansas, doctor explained. "I can't be for sure, but I believe you are going to have twins. Your feet and legs are swollen to a most dangerous level. You could lose your babies and maybe your own life. You must stay off your feet."

"But Doctor, I must take care of my family. I can't go to bed." Nancy replied.

"Nancy, you let me and the Doc worry about that," Jess Stokes reassured his wife. "I'm sure I can get my sister, Annie to come stay with us and take care of you and our family."

Annie was overjoyed to help with Nancy's confinement and take care of their two living children, Carl Emmit and La Vern. Times were very difficult. Many children died at birth while others took pneumonia at an early age or died from other diseases.

The Stokes twins made their appearance a few days short of the scheduled nine months and weighed nine pounds each. Claude was born first with Clyde being born fifteen minutes later. It was understandable that their mother had to be confined to bed and had to remain in bed for one month after their birth.

Annie was a very good nurse and bonded quickly to the babies as she cared for their every need. As she was bathing one of the identical twins she came running to Nancy's bedside very excited.

"Look! Nancy I know a way to tell these boys apart."

"What do you ever mean Annie?" Nancy asked.

"See, this baby has two crooked little fingers."

As Nancy was nursing the twin with the crooked fingers, Annie left the room to bathe the second twin. She came back in only a few minutes and said; "You can forget telling them apart because this baby has crooked little fingers too."

* * *

World War I began in August of 1914. However, the United States did not enter the war until April 6, 1917. Some historians say World War II was a continuation of World War I, with only twenty years between the two, and both were fought in Europe against the most powerful nation of Germany.[1]

* * *

Jess Whitmore Stokes, father of Claude and Clyde was on his way to be inducted into the Army on November 11, 1919, when Germany signed the armistice. His train was stopped and he returned home to his wife and two young sons, Carl and Harvey. He did not serve in World War I, but he was to see Carl, Claude, and Clyde serve in World War II.

The Great Depression engulfed the United States, as it did the nations of Europe during the period of reconstruction after World War I.

Jess Whitmore age 22

Deep discontentment arose in the United States, brought on by the worst economic depression in history, sweeping Franklin D. Roosevelt into the Presidency. [2]

The Jess Stokes family lived in Dierks, Arkansas, in the early lives of the Stokes twins. He worked in the lumber and farming industry. Because of stressful economic conditions, Father Stokes began looking for better opportunities in providing for his family, causing him to move them to Tishomingo, in a thriving farming community located in south central, Oklahoma. The principal crop was cotton. The twins were approximately two years old when they moved to Oklahoma.

Narrow escapes from death for the Stokes twins occurred throughout their lives, including World War II. Mother Stokes told of their harrowing escapes quite often. Their first fiasco happened when they lived in Tishomingo. Most of the family were in the cotton field working and had left the five-year-old boys playing in a side room built on the house, containing special cotton Mother Stokes was saving for quilt batting. Clyde found some cigarettes, which his Uncle Sim Stokes had been smoking. Being curious, he attempted to light one, burning his finger. He threw the match into the cotton causing flames to quickly engulf the house. The frightened boys ran from the house into a nearby wooded area to hide.

Meanwhile, the Stokes family saw the smoke and frantically ran to the burning house, thinking the two boys were still inside. By the time they reached the house everything was burned to the ground which made it impossible to rescue the boys. As they were telling this experience, the question was asked, "When you came out of hiding, did Mother Stokes paddle you?" Clyde answered, "No, she was so happy to see us alive, but it sure taught us a good lesson, never to smoke again." In fact, none of the Stokes family ever took up the habit of smoking.

About a year later another incident took place when they lived in Tishomingo. The twins were hiding as they watched their Uncle Sim hide a jar of whiskey, and when their uncle left the barn, the boys got the whiskey. Clyde decided he would taste it. He continued to have a little sip and got drunk.

Finally, the boys went into the house. Claude was trying to hold Clyde upright as he staggered into the kitchen where Mother

Stokes was preparing a meal. Clyde stuttered with a slur to his speech and a very thick tongue, "Mama, let me sell you a good team of mules." Mother Stokes, with much shock in her voice declared, "Clyde, you're drunk! Young man you go to bed, I'm going to spank you when you sober up."

Mother Stokes frequently used the rod of discipline, usually spanking both boys. She sometimes included their sister La Vern, as she was often with the boys in their mischief. "That way I knew I was getting the right one," she explained.

The following morning Claude told Clyde that he was going to get spanked for drinking 'that' whiskey. Clyde went into the kitchen where his mother was preparing breakfast and told her how ashamed he was for drinking. Mother Stokes didn't have the heart to spank him, but instructed Claude to take Clyde into the bedroom and lecture him.

Mother Stokes told of Claude's encounter with Clyde. There was a picture of an angel hanging on the wall. Claude said, "Clyde, do you see that angel? If you drink whiskey you never will get to be an angel." Clyde thought a minute and retorted, "Shoot! I never wanted to be one anyway." The boys learned another good lesson, never to drink intoxicating beverages. Neither one ever drank again.

Mother Stokes was a great disciplinarian with all her children. She believed one should not spare the rod and spoil the child. She never spanked a child in anger, but waited sometimes hours later, to administer punishment. Claude admitted, "It would not have been so bad if she just paddled us and got it over with, but we had to dread it for half a day and we knew she was not going to forget her promise to punish."

In 1931 or 32, Claude and Clyde moved with their family to Indianola, Oklahoma. The Stokes family lived on the 'Perkins' place, and continued to farm as tenants. This community became known for raising great Bermuda onions.

The Stokes family moved closer to McAlester, when they moved from Indianola to Scipio. This area was known as Whiskey Bottom; surrounded by beautiful rugged mountains, and plush farming valleys, where the Canadian River flowed in and out through a picturesque location. Whiskey Bottom was a moon-shiners paradise for making Wild Cat Whiskey, which was an illegal product. Claude said, "The only way you could get into those mountains to check on the whiskey stills was by horse back. All those men engaged in the illegal profession protected each other, to keep law enforcement officers from finding and destroying their way of making money.

(picture on the right)
**Carrie Campbell overlooking
Canadian River and mountains**

"As the whiskey making was going on, we were farming the land and raising animals to provide food for the family. Papa Stokes never made whiskey to sell, but he did try his hand at making some for his own use, which he claimed was for medicinal purposes."

Claude and Clyde began their education in Indianola at the age of seven. They later attended school in Scipio at Rocky Point School for two years. Claude commented, "I remember our teacher, Professor Grey was up in years and each day, in the one-room school house, he took a nap and gave us a book to read. I always read *Freddy Shoveled Away the Snow.*

Jaunita Lott Maisano, a good friend in our church, also attended school with the twins. She tells the amusing story of how the two boys played cowboys while Professor Grey was taking his nap. They ran quite a distance across the room and jumped astride the long wood-burning stove, riding the make-believe horse.

Claude related, "Pauline Johnson later became our teacher and lived with our family, as this was the custom in those days. One day, she instructed me to throw away my only stick of gum I was chewing. I tossed my gum out of the

Clyde, Teacher, and Claude

open window onto a board. At recess I went outside and retrieved my gum, which resulted in Miss Johnson giving me the only paddling I ever received in school. Needless to say, I received another spanking from Mom when I got home. Parents cooperated with teachers in this manner as students were corrected "

The Stokes family moved from Scipio, to Mitchell School District, on a farm located seven miles northwest of McAlester on Route 1. The farm was east of the landmark, 'Coal Creek Bridge', which led the way to McAlester Lake. The family farmed one hundred acres of rich, fertile land for growing crops and pasturing their cattle. The farm was rented from James S. Arnote, a prominent lawyer, in McAlester. Their principal crop was corn.

Mr. Arnote not only owned the Stokes farm but adjacent properties as well. Joe Anderson managed a chicken ranch, and L. L. Goatcher operated a dairy.

Claude said, "The Anderson and Goatcher families became our life-long friends. We often exchanged work with one another. Every Sunday, Mr. Arnote came to see all three families, as we supplied him with fruits, vegetables, chickens, eggs, milk, and butter."

In 1934, the Stokes children began attending school in Mitchell School District, with approximately seventy-five students, being taught by Ruth Savage and Helen Evans. A pot-bellied, wood burning stove heated the two-room school. The Stokes children walked three and one-half miles to and from school each day in all kinds of weather. Each morning as the children arrived they were lined up outside, single file, and marched into the class rooms where they stood at attention saluted and pledged allegiance to the United States Flag, and sang, *My country, 'tis, of Thee.*

Runion of Mitchell School Graduates Ruth Stacks, Dorene Goatcher , Ruth Savage (teacher), Frances Anderson

Claude confessed, "Teachers used a paddle to enforce good behavior. Miss Ruth was very small in stature, but she often spanked a twenty-year old young man who was still attending her class. Some older students who attended class had, at some time, dropped out of class to help on their family farm."

Claude and Clyde had great fun playing sports, especially basketball. Claude said, with a twinkle in his eye, "We were in a basketball tournament and one of us was about to foul out of the game. At half time Miss Ruth, who was coaching, took us to the dressing room and changed our shirts. The referees never knew the difference."

In the early years of Claude and Clyde's lives there were no modern conveniences such as running water, inside bath facilities, or electricity.

Claude said, "Our Mom was a great old saint and homemaker, as she labored with patience, carrying water from springs to do the family washings. Wood was burned under a huge black pot where the water was heated to the boiling point. Clothes were rubbed on a rub-board and boiled in the pot. Finally the clothes were rubbed again, rinsed, and hung out to dry on any kind of line she might find available.

"We saw times when animals broke out of their fence and ran into the clothes, dragging them through the dirt. Of course the washing had to be done over.

"After the washing was completed, the boiling water from the pot was used, with lye added, to scrub all the pine floors in the house. This sterilized the floors and turned them into a beautiful golden color. Ironing was done with old flat irons heated on the wood cook stove. We didn't have lawn mowers in those days. The dirt yards were swept clean with a broom. Weeds were cut down, but Mom

always planted and raised beautiful flowers." **Claude, Mother, Clyde**

Mother Stokes helped the family plant and harvest fruits and vegetables, which she preserved by canning them in a huge pressure cooker. She also canned beef, pork sausage, fish, and even wild game.

There was no refrigeration and no other way to keep food, except when they were able to purchase pounds of block ice from McAlester and store it in a wooden icebox, which only kept ice for a short time.

Mother Stokes taught her daughters to help her in crafts, such as piecing quilts and then quilting them to make covers for the family. Papa Stokes purchased her a treadle Singer sewing machine that she used in making clothes for the family. She did not buy material by the yard, but made dresses for herself and the girls from colorful flour sacks she had saved.

Papa Stokes was a good provider and taught his boys to farm, hunt for wild game, trap animals for furs, gig for frog legs, and fish in the old Coal Creek, which ran through the farm. He also taught the boys to care for the many cattle, hogs, chickens, turkeys, and other animals on the farm.

Claude said, "I can remember when we had twenty cows to milk by hand, both in the morning and evening. The milk was separated and then taken to McAlester, where it was sold to the cheese factory.

Clyde and Claude

Age 15

"Papa taught us to do many farm chores. He taught us to kill hogs; which included butchering, curing, and hanging the meat in a smokehouse for safe keeping through the winter.

"We also learned to make lye soap by using the animal fat, lye, and other special ingredients. This soap was used for everything, including washing clothes, cleaning floors, taking baths, and was a pretty good thing to use for the seven-year itch. I might add, our Mom did use that lye soap to wash out our mouths for using bad words.

"We spent many hours cutting down trees and clearing the virgin land, previously owned by the Indians. The wood was cut and sized with crosscut saws and chopping axes to fit cook stoves, heaters, and fireplaces. After enough wood was cut for the winter, we were allowed to cut wood and sell to anyone who wished to purchase it. The money we made was ours to keep and this gave us soda pop money. We got the big sum of one dollar for each rick of wood, thinking we were making big money."

Each member of the Stokes family shared in the chores to be done. There was dignity in being able to contribute one's part of the work. Claude explained, "We didn't think we were poor, because our neighbors endured hard times by sharing with one another. Actually, in those days of depression, we never went hungry. We had a warm place to live, loving parents, many friends, good schools, and enjoyed creating our own entertainment on the farm. Many people who lived in towns or cities did not do nearly as well through the depression days."

These years became the most formative years of their lives. Obedience and respect for their parents was very important in building their character and moral values.

Claude said, "I only remember Papa Jess whipping us one time, and I can't remember what it was for. We just knew to obey, or suffer the consequences."

Mr. Arnote and the twins had a mutual admiration and respect for each other. He was very influential in their character building in those young years. The boys took great pride in showing him around the farm, pointing out all the new animals and crops. He was a very frugal man and taught the boys the meaning of saving their money. Claude said, "I can remember him saying, 'Boys, always watch out for your pennies and the dollars will take care of themselves.' "

One day he bought a new car and proceeded to drive the boys around the farm. Claude noticed he never shifted the gears from second into high.

"Mr Arnote, don't you ever put this thing in high?" Claude asked.

"It runs so good in medium," he explained, "I forget to put her in high."

In the late 1930's, during the winter, the Stokes house caught on fire and burned with the family barely escaping. Mr. Arnote came to their rescue again as he had the house re-built in a very short time, helping with the construction himself. He taught the boys how to drive nails properly while they were roofing the house.

Claude said, "I was holding the hammer down near the head of the hammer, when Mr. Arnote took the hammer, and taught us how to hold on the far end as we nailed the nails into a board.   I taught that same lesson to our grandsons, Chad and Brent Harris, four years ago, as they helped me build our fence around the yard.

"Work on the farm was very hard as we learned to walk behind a team of mules to plow. I recall Papa Jess purchased two mules from a nearby farmer, Mr. Robbins.   Clyde and I went to get those young unbroken mules, thinking we knew exactly what to do.   Well, we decided to unhitch our old team and tie them on to the back of the wagon, putting harness on the new team and hitching them to the wagon.   One of us held the reins and the other one held on to the brake, and the race was on.   Those mules ran as fast as they could go, finally giving completely out, after running for the distance of five miles to our home.   Cars and other teams on the road hit ditches on both sides, trying to avoid those crazy mules running over them. Wow! What fun!

"Mr. Robbins, at a later date said, 'Mr. Stokes, I just knew those crazy boys were going to be killed, pulling that stunt.'"   He didn't know those twins had the time of their lives taking big chances; therefore creating joyful entertainment for themselves.

Claude and Clyde seemed to get their greatest thrill from living on the farm by training and riding their horses, and farming with the mules.   They gave names to their animals such as; Nip and Tuck; Red and Blue, and Tub and Rodie.

Red, Clyde and Blue

Claude was asked, "How do you spell Rodie?"

"I don't know," he replied, "I never did ask him how to spell it. I just said it."   This was a typical answer one might receive from him.

Claude related, "One day Clyde and I were cutting wood about three quarters of a mile from the house. Tub and Rodie, were standing near-by, hitched to the wagon.   All of a sudden they became spooked from something and began to run away.   The wheels started hitting cut stumps in their pathway, which scared them more.   They ran so hard, hitting many stumps, causing the wagon bed to go flying in one direction, and the back wheels in another. When Tub and Rodie got near the house, with only the two front wheels still connected to the mules, Mom just knew we had been killed. She and La Vern came running to find us. We were folded over in laughter. When we saw Mom in tears, it wasn't quite so funny.

"Later, Clyde and I, with some other boys, were cutting and hauling wood from a near-by area, not too far from the house, when an incident took place involving our horses Nip and Tuck. As the horses were standing hitched to the wagon, Clyde opened the gate to drive them through. Clyde said, 'Whoa'. The horses headed in a dead run to the house,

Tub, Claude and Rodie

going between the house and barn, running over one of our best milk cows, and skinning her up from head to foot.

"After that day, we could walk up where that old cow was chewing her cud, rattle the wooden fence, and she would go nuts, thinking she was about to be run over again. She never did give over a gallon of milk a day after that run-a-way."

Claude and Clyde enjoyed racing with other farm boys with their horses and teams. They lined up at Coal Creek Bridge and raced their horses to Pumpkin Center, located at the fork of the road where roads led to Lake McAlester and Scipio. Whoever reached the finished line first was treated at the near-by small country store, with an R. C. Cola, and a Big Dip, or Baby Ruth candy bar. When they were asked, "How much did those things cost?" Claude answered, "You could get the pop for five cents and the candy bar for five cents. One day we went in to the store when Lee Phillips owned it and bought all the goodies he had. This made him mad because he didn't have anything left to sell.

"Finally our mode of farming started changing from mules to tractors. We first used a John Deere tractor as we made levees and dug ponds on Mr. Arnote's farm. Papa Jess, eventually bought us a Massey Harris, and then an International tractor to use in the late

1930's. We thought we hit big time with those tractors; however we did not have as many laughs as we did with mules. Farming became easier for us as new equipment was being invented and was made available to us.

"In 1936 a tremendous drought prevailed in Oklahoma. The ponds, wells, creeks, and rivers were dry. In the Mitchell Community our only source of water was from a spring southwest of Coal Creek Bridge. After a days work in the fields, all the farmers raced their teams and wagons to the spring to haul barrels of water for family use. We loved the thrill and challenge as we participated in the big race.

"In the late 1930's, Clyde and I worked as janitors at Mitchell School and earned enough money to purchase our family's first radio. It was a Philco radio with A and B batteries. Our favorite program was Lum and Abner. Folks from miles around came to hear our radio. This was quite an invention. We had to be careful not to play it too long at one time, as the batteries would run down.

"In the day time, women listened to programs like Ma Perkins and Stella Dallas. One day I went to the L. L. Goatcher Ranch, while we were bailing hay for him. When I got to their house, I found all the women crying up a storm. I asked them what was wrong.

" ' Someone just poisoned Stella Dallas,' " Dorene replied.

"Boy, did I laugh at them; which resulted in their running me off, causing me to forget why I had gone to their house.

"It could have been wire for the hay baling we were doing. We had gone on strike for higher pay. Mr. Goatcher was paying us ten cents per ton and we asked for eleven cents. We learned, later in life, we had gone on a strike. Folks did not know anything about strikes in those days. We began baling thirty bales of hay for eleven cents as Mr. Goatcher was forced to meet our request."

The Stokes family home was always open to adults as well as young people to have fun and enjoy being together. Claude said, "I remember we usually had a big crowd to eat with us on Sunday. Mom and La Vern never knew for how many they were preparing dinner. If we needed more food, we just wrung another old chicken's head off. Everyone was always made to feel welcome. The Stokes family seemed to draw a big crowd of young people on any occasion."

Entertainment for the twins took place in their home and homes of friends. Some friends gave community-swinging parties, which was walking around the room to guitar and fiddle music. The music could not be considered real music, or the swinging game as genuine dancing, but the young people and adults had fun participating.

Adult chaperoning was a part of their life style. Claude bragged a little by saying, "The Jones family had two pretty daughters. The boys tried to date them, but Mrs. Jones always insisted that she walk a few steps behind them with a lighted, oil lantern. I solved that problem in a hurry. I managed a date with the prettiest Jones daughter. I walked up to the door and knocked. When Mrs. Jones answered the door, I told her how happy I was to walk her and the daughter to the party. Mrs. Jones, trusting me completely, quietly asked to be excused and let us go without her. The other boys never did know how I managed that date.

"More modern entertainment started appearing as picture shows became popular. We country boys rode our horses into McAlester on Saturday to see movies selected from five movie theaters. The theaters showed a feature movie, a serial, and a comedy.

Most all the movies were the Western variety, starring movie stars like, Gene Autry and Frog Millhouse, Roy Rogers and Dale Evans, Tex Ritter, and others. The continued serial, I can remember, was Tom Mix. We could hardly wait, to go back each week, to see what happened to Tom Mix and his horse as they had plunged over a cliff from the previous week.

"Sometimes, there were as many as six or eight boys on horseback to see the movies. Late in the evening we usually went by Allison's Drug Store, and bought all the bananas the owner had left. Most of the time, we bought a whole stalk, hung them on a pole, and carried them between two horses. Before we traveled the seven miles to Coal Creek Bridge, we ate all the bananas and left a trail of peelings up and down the road."

Clyde confessed, "Mom didn't know how we managed to go to the picture show when we rode our horses into McAlester. The show cost ten cents. I bought the ticket to see the complete movie, and then Claude asked the usher to let him go in and find me. We exchanged places and I came out thanking the usher. We both saw the movie for ten cents."

Evidently, Mother Stokes did not know some of their tricks, as that behavior did not meet her standards for honesty and integrity.

Coal Creek Bridge remains as a landmark in the Mitchell Community. Directions to all parts of the country can be given by using Coal Creek Bridge as a starting point.

COAL CREEK BRIDGE

Recently, Claude was asked to give a speech on *Who Am I*, in his Sunday School Department, of First Baptist Church. Of course, he had to tell the following story, in his amusing way. "At the end of Coal Creek Bridge, on the west-side of the road, still stands a native rock house and that is the place I first met my future wife. An old boy went to McAlester and brought a carload of girls to a swinging party at this house. Looking all the little fillies over, I saw this cute little blonde and said to myself, I've just got to get her out on Coal Creek Bridge. We played games like 'Good Night Go Walking'. She was blindfolded and chose me to walk with her instead of the other guy. While we were walking the first time, I told her I would press her hand three times, as a signal, so I would get to walk with her across the bridge again and again. I walked her across the bridge several times and showed her the moon and stars. She never did get over it. Well, I guess she did too, for after three months of dating her, with her two older brothers, Aubrey and Doyle Epps tagging along, she quit me."

The story has a happy ending because Claude proposed to me, by letter, while he was in Europe fighting in World War II. We were married on March 27, 1945, when Claude was home on his first forty-five day furlough before the war ended in May of 1945.

Claude and Clyde started fighting before they entered World War II. Boxing was a very popular sport. They entered prizefights held in McAlester in the days of Max Baer, Billy Conn, and Joe Lewis. Claude said, "we entered the 'free for all', involving five guys in the ring at one time. The one who remained in the ring till the end, without being knocked down, was declared the winner and received $2.00. Clyde and I would gang up on the other three, resulting in our being the last two standing. That beat cutting wood.

"Fighting other boys in the communities of Mitchell, Blue, Tannehill, and Bug Tussle also took place. The fighting usually erupted when we rode our horses to a community party, in one of those locations, and flirted with someone's girl.

"The guys at Blue fought with knucks, made from tub handles, Tannehill fought with small pieces of trace chain, and Bug Tussle, (school of Carl Albert-former speaker of the house) fought with five-cell flash lights. We didn't fight with those things. We fought fair. However, after a big fight at Blue, I decided to make me a pair of tub handle knucks. I took them with me the next time we went to Blue. The first punch got me, when I knocked the hide off all my knuckles. Mom never did know what happened to the handles off her number three washtub."

In viewing the early lives of the Stokes Twins one may see how important early upbringing was, and is, in the lives of young people. Many people have contributed to the success of these two young men, as they grew into heroes of their nation, and later into responsible, Godly citizens, Christians, and fathers. Great acknowledgment goes to the parents who guided their lives, teachers who taught them, friends who supported and befriended them, plus others who lifted them up in prayer while they were fighting for their country.

Even though they did not have formal education, their wisdom and dedication to God, family, and nation far out-weighed their lack of education. The twins were taught to work and count it as a blessing, to play and have fun, to love and be loved, to have empathy for the less fortunate, and to reach out to those in need.

In the late 1930's Claude and Clyde continued to help their father on the Stokes farm near McAlester, Oklahoma. However, many farmers left their farms to find work elsewhere as production of war materials increased.

Conditions in the United States began to improve as thousands of factories, ammunition plants, and shipyards began making supplies for the Allies. Many families left the farm to improve their living conditions as they traveled across the United States to find employment. The men were often separated from their families for lengthy times as migration took place.

Parents across the nation could well remember World War II and the sacrifices that had to be made. The dread of their sons going to a foreign land to fight for freedom was ever present as storm clouds continued to form across the world.

Many young people can still remember parents sitting near a radio with tear-filled eyes as they listened to the appeal of Great Britain for help as Hitler was threatening their beloved country. Yet the spirit of patriotism reached an all-time high as our nation realized war was inevitable for our people. Not only did most Americans show an overwhelming loyalty to our nation, but to all freedom loving nations, especially, Great Britain and France.

Prime Minister Winston Churchill was a persistent and eloquent speaker as he rallied his countrymen to fight to the very end to defend England with these words:

"Never give up!"…

"We shall not flag or fail. We shall go on to the end. We shall fight in France, we shall   fight on the seas and oceans, we shall fight with growing confidence and growing strength in the air, we shall defend our island, whatever the cost may be, we shall fight on the beaches, we shall fight on the landing grounds, we shall fight in the fields and in the streets, we shall fight in the hills; we shall never surrender!"[3]

Claude and Clyde continued to work on their farm until they reached the age to be accepted in the armed forces. During the 1940's, *Boogie Woogie* music and dancing became very popular._ Across the nation, young people and servicemen enjoyed many popular bands: Tommy Dorsey, Jimmy Goodman, Glenn Miller, and others.   The Stokes twins enjoyed going to the American Legion Building on Saturday nights to hear Bob Wills and his Texas Playboys. Bob Wills added, " auh-haw", on the end of his music. Claude can imitate Bob's vocal signature quite well. His favorite Western song was, and is, *Milk Cow Blues.*

Prior to Claude and Clyde's entrance into service Claude tells about their last narrow escapes.

"Most of the boys in the country had a saddle horse. All of us wanted to have the fastest horse so we could win races from Coal

Creek Bridge to Pumpkin Center Grocery Store. The winner was awarded with a R. C. Cola and a candy bar. I usually won the races because Shorty, my horse, was fast as a bullet. However, there was only one thing wrong with Shorty, after winning the race, he kept running and was very hard for me to bring him to a stop. This led to Shorty's down fall.

"One Saturday, late in the afternoon as the sun was going down, a group of six or eight boys were riding into McAlester, when one of the boys challenged me to race his new horse. I told him I didn't want to race down the open road. He bragged by saying, 'Come on Claude, my horse can beat old Shorty. You are afraid I will win'. So I finally agreed to run the race. Shorty won the race but I couldn't get him stopped. We were going up a small hill in the road and when we came over the hill a car with lights on suddenly appeared. As the lights hit Shorty in the face, he was unable to see. I couldn't pull him to the left or to the right. The car was going forty miles per hour. So were Shorty and I when we hit head-on. I went thirty feet in the air still in the saddle as I came down in the middle of the road. I received skinned knees and a sprained wrist from the fall, but the accident killed old Shorty as dead as a doornail.

Shorty, Gerald, and Floyd Deweese

The car was totaled and the driver of the car spent a week in the hospital. Oh well, that was just a part of being a country boy. I escaped death again.

"Two weeks later, I was riding on the front fender of a 1936 Ford. I was perched on one fender with a girl on the other side. A coon hunter in a pickup loaded with hound dogs pulled out in front of the car. When we ran into the back of the pickup, I threw my feet up and rammed them through a one by twelve board on the dog cage. The only injury I received was blistered feet from the impact, but the fender on which I was riding was completely torn off. The girl on the other fender was almost killed, and stayed in the hospital for some time. I escaped serious injury again.

"Clyde also had some mishaps. He was driving our Dad's new tractor, when for no reason, he ran head-on into a tree while I was hollering for him to pull over. I think he was daydreaming about his girl. He wasn't hurt seriously."

Claude, after all the accidents occurring in such a short period of time said, "Clyde, we are now eighteen. I think its time for us to join the army where it's safe. We are going to get killed on this dangerous farm."

-2-

World War II Training

In the summer of 1940, General George C. Marshall, Army Chief of Staff announced the danger of the United States of America being invaded. He stated that our country could not be defended without an army being raised by conscription or draft. The Selective Service Act became law on September 16, 1940, and by the end of January 1, 1942, one million men were in the armed services of our country.[1]

Carl, the Stokes twin's older brother, volunteered into the National Guard of the 45th Division in the late 1930's. The 45th Division was mobilized on September 16, 1940, prior to the twins' entrance into military service.

On December 7, 1941, the Japanese bombed Pearl Harbor, plunging the United States into World War II. Claude and Clyde were only seventeen years old and still helping their father on the Arnote Farm. Carl's 45th Division was in training for their mobilization, destined to fight in the European Theater of War.

Jess W. Stokes, father of Claude and Clyde, had great concern for the welfare of his family. He realized the twins had never spent a night away from each other in all their years of growing up in the Stokes home.

Prior to the twins volunteering into the armed forces Papa Stokes decided he would write to President Franklin D. Roosevelt and ask that the twins be allowed to stay together.

He was aware that a law had been passed that brothers were not allowed to serve together because of the tragic deaths of the five

Sullivan brothers, serving together on board the *USS Juneau* (sunk on November 13, 1942).

Claude said, "I remember people laughing and saying, 'Mr. Stokes, the President of the United States will not pay any attention to an old dirt farmer like you. You are wasting your time.' "

"Papa retorted, ' I'll just write and prove to you, that he is the leader I think he is. He has never failed us farmers yet.'"

"President Roosevelt had a great love for the farmers and those less fortunate in our nation. In only a few short weeks he responded and granted Papa his request to keep Clyde and I together for the duration of our military service. To insure that this command was obeyed, the President ordered us to carry a copy of his letter with us."

Claude and Clyde volunteered to the draft board in McAlester, Oklahoma on November 18, 1942. They were anxious to get into the service and perform their duty as American citizens. However, they had to wait until an ample number of men in Pittsburg County were recruited before the group was transported to Tulsa, Oklahoma for their physical examinations. After passing the physical they were given a serial number, sworn in, and inducted into the armed service of the United States on January 14, 1943.

They were instructed to return home for seven days and get their business in order. Claude said, "We didn't have much business; just milk the old cows again, say good-bye to the farm, our parents, sisters, LaVern and Eupal, and of course kiss all the crying girls good-bye".

Mother Stokes, LaVern and Eupal

Imagine if you will, these twins were leaving home for the very first time, had only seen three of the forty-eight states of our nation; Arkansas, Oklahoma and Texas.

After seven days at home, getting their business in order, approximately one hundred-fifty volunteers and draftees were transported by bus from McAlester to Fort Sill, Oklahoma.

"It was a cold winter day when we arrived, and the wind was blowing like crazy," Claude explained.

"We looked out to see huge tents scattered over the vast area where recruits were housed. Each tent held about twenty men. In the center of

Caravan of Army Trucks

the tent was a big pot-bellied, wood stove that some of us had to keep wood in through the night. Not quite the comforts of home, but Clyde and I were familiar with farm living and we were tough.

"Fort Sill was an evacuation center for the purpose of determining which branch of service each man was most qualified. A man could choose to serve in the United States Army, Navy, Air Force, Marine Corps, Coast Guard, and others. The interviewing officer considered a man's preference, education, and previous occupation. After three days of filling out papers, and answering questions, the officer in charge determined from our experience on the farm; operating tractors and other heavy equipment, we were most qualified to serve in the Armored Force, of the United States Army."

For the first time the officer in charge informed the twins that they would have to be separated.

Clyde immediately advised, "I believe you might need to look at this," as he handed him the letter. When the officer read the letter, he was stunned to see it was signed by President Franklin D. Roosevelt. After much consideration he returned the letter and instructed them to present the letter to future commanding officers.

"We left Fort Sill, fully dressed in army uniforms and given a duffel bag containing additional clothing," Claude commented.

"Fort Knox, Kentucky was our next training center. Lines of wooden barracks came into view and after appropriate papers were presented we were ordered to advance. We began to feel as if we were really in the army, especially after seeing several groups of around sixty men marching in uniform with rifles on their shoulders. A loud sergeant was bellowing out orders. Clyde drawled, ' I bet we get the meanest sergeant on the base.' "

All the recruits were unloaded and ordered to line up. Each man was assigned to a company, a platoon, and barracks. Claude explained, "We were assigned to Company B, 3rd Platoon of the 13th Armored Replacement Battalion with Lt. Col. B. R. Moore as Battalion Commander, First Lieut. H. E. Crow as Commander of Company B, and Liut. Seprell as Commander of the Third Platoon.

"The sergeant of our barracks instructed us to follow him. I can't say the sergeant was mean but he was quite thorough in telling us we were to shape up, keep our clothes neatly in the foot locker at the end of our assigned bed, and make those bed sheets pop. He demanded cleanliness, shoes shined, rifles cleaned, barracks always in order, and to be ready for inspection at all times. We were instructed to stand at attention until we were dismissed and to salute all officers. He informed us that he was in charge of our barracks and we would obey his orders as he expected us to become the best platoon in the United States Army.

"As we were dismissed we became aware of not only Oklahoma and Texas men, but men from other states especially those from New York and New Jersey. Texans, we could understand but those 'Yanks', well that was another question. Some of those guys had never experienced having their feet on soil. They had been accustomed to the concrete streets of New York. Many had never seen a real live cow. Boy! They were something else.

"We learned they were also getting impressions of us. They thought we were still fighting Indians in Oklahoma. Some of them had never shot a gun or rifle. Clyde and I were steps ahead of them, we thought, as being raised on the farm had given us the advantage in shooting, fighting, and enduring tough situations. Looking back, we can see how accepting other people not exactly like us was God's plan for our lives in maturing and becoming men worthy of being called Americans.

"The bugle call marked the daily routine in army camps. *Taps* announced the end of our first day as the bugle echoed throughout the camp. At 10:00 o'clock in the evening all lights were out and we were to be in bed. It didn't seem too long a night, until we heard the bugle again playing *Reveille* for waking-up-time. We had a few short minutes to get dressed, make our beds, and stand at attention.

"On the first morning the sergeant directed us to the mess hall for army chow. We found the army had good food and plenty of it. At times we were required to do some form of exercise such as push-ups, two-mile hikes, or marching before we could go to chow. In the army you did as you were ordered with no questions asked. After a few days, soldiers learned to keep well fed as the push-ups and other exercises ate up energy in a hurry.

"That first day was to be a nightmare for some. The sergeant ordered our men to report for haircuts. Some of those guys had pretty wavy hair and had it combed so, so. As they sat down in the barber's chair, the barber asked them how they wanted it cut. The army barber played around for a little and then went straight over the top of their heads with clippers, giving them what was known as a 'GI haircut.' Some of those guys actually cried. It didn't bother Clyde and me; we were accustomed to a bad haircut. We could remember when a barber in McAlester asked us if we wanted wavy hair and when we answered 'yes', he just cut gaps straight around our heads and called it wavy." Even now, Claude sometimes yearns for a good old GI haircut, and did get one, one time.

Shortly after the twins arrived at Fort Knox, Claude recalls this humorous story. "Clyde and I, and another soldier were walking across the parade grounds when we met a colonel and a major. Clyde and I saluted the officers, but the other soldier did not salute. The major turned to the soldier and barked, 'Soldier, how long you been in the army?' The soldier answered back, 'Three days, how long you guys been in?' The officers glanced at each other, and went away snickering.

Claude, Pat Williams and Clyde-

They apparently could not keep a straight face to reprimand the soldier for not saluting them."

The Stokes twins have vivid memories concerning the phases of their military training. Claude related, "At the time of our actual training we did not fully realize how important that training was, until later, when we stood in battle confronted with decisions we had to make. Our following the instructions we were given in training saved our lives many times.

"The sergeant in charge started us out with marching drills with calls like; 'March, left, right, halt, right flank, left flank, and to the rear march'. At times he would drill in a singing voice, 'left, left, I had a good home but I left.' Many soldiers could not distinguish the right from the left foot. I recall two soldiers from Tennessee who were really great guys, but could never learn to march. We spent a lot of time trying to teach them right from left. We put a stick in one hand and a rock in the other, but nothing worked.

"They were eventually released from the Army because they could not learn to march. We regretted them leaving the service because of that technicality. We knew how much they wanted to serve their country. Clyde and I thought that was harsh then, but when we got into battle we saw how important those commands were. For instance, if a commanding officer told Clyde to turn our tank right and he turned left, not following that order could have caused us to lose the tank and six valuable soldiers.

"Marching with precision was a great thing to see. Many times the commanding officer observed the sergeants with their platoons as they practiced short order drills. Our sergeant trained some men in the platoon to lead the drill in his place. The soldiers were to march on a platform about 60` x 60`. As the orders were called out, many times, the one leading the drill would make a mistake and the soldiers walked off the platform. This made for a lot of laughs but they eventually caught on to the drilling.

"The greatest marching I ever saw was by a black quartermaster company. Those black marching soldiers were great to watch, with their singsong and quick precision marching.

"We enjoyed our training on the firing range. Each soldier had to qualify in firing three major guns: pistols, rifles, and machine guns. We were given the guns and a target was set up.

We had ten rounds of ammunition and when we fired into the center circle the required number of times we were qualified.

"Field range firing was more difficult. Trainees were required to fire at moving figures as they popped up in unexpected places. Our ability to hit those moving targets was recorded. Some of the 'Yanks' had never fired a gun. It took many of them several days to qualify. Clyde and I qualified right off because we were accustomed to hunting for wild game.

"The Yanks thought we were sure-shots because we had practice in fighting Indians. Funny, how people get those strange ideas. They didn't know it, but we were two of those Cherokee Indians, at least, one-eighth.

"The escapades of our brother, Carl who was in the 45th Division, could have created some of those ideas. I recall him telling of being in a New York restaurant before he went overseas. Carl, Schilcht Billy who was a full blood Choctaw Indian and several other soldiers of the 45th were ordering food. When it came Schilcht Billy's turn to order, he startled the waitress by saying, "' Me want buffalo meat.' "

"The waitress replied, 'Sorry, we do not have buffalo meat.' "

" 'Bring big bowl turtle soup,' " Schilcht Billy demanded. As she told him they did not have any turtle soup, he got up and did a war dance, half scaring her to death. The men got a big kick out of trying to make those 'Yanks' think the war with Indians was still going on." Carl was very much like Claude, as he enjoyed creating a humorous situation.

Claude continued. "Classes were given in map, coordinate, and compass reading. We usually came in out of the cold into a warm classroom and tried to stay awake for the class, but we didn't give our full attention to the training because we became sleepy. It didn't seem too important at the time. It reminds me of growing up at home. We thought our Dad was an old fogy when he tried to teach us some things, but when we grew up, we found out he was a lot smarter than we thought. When we got overseas and had to read those maps we were given, we wished we had been more alert in map classes.

"We were taught to respect all army vehicles. If we used a vehicle such as a truck, jeep, or other equipment, the vehicle was checked out to us and before returning it, the vehicle had to be washed and cleaned before it could be checked in.

"We learned to drive all vehicles; jeeps, motorcycles, trucks of all kinds, and tanks. I recall a humorous story about learning to ride a motorcycle.

"The training track was in the form of a circle with a track going around, inside a chain-link fence, which was twelve feet high. The drill sergeant had about fifteen of us out for instruction. As each trainee came forward for his turn at learning how to operate the vehicle, the sergeant aligned himself on the inside, atop a motorcycle, and instructed the trainee to align himself, on the outside of him, on a motorcycle. The sergeant instructed each one through the same maneuver.

"As one trainee got on the motorcycle, the sergeant barked, 'Start the engine like this; put it in gear, go slow, and now rev it up, not too much now, slow it down, now get a little faster, slow it down, rev it up a little more'... All of sudden the trainee got excited, and pushed the gas full force. The motorcycle and trainee flew around the course, going ninety to nothing. The chase was on. The sergeant had completely lost control of the situation.

"'Halt!' 'Let up on the gas!' 'Stop!' The sergeant yelled, as he cut across the area, trying to stop the recruit. The sergeant finally gave up in desperation.

"Prior to this time, we had never seen such a display of acrobatic entertainment. All of a sudden the trainee, atop the motorcycle, started going around the fence so fast, the tires on his vehicle seemed to be glued to the fence. The recruit was holding on for dear life, but still going around and around the fence. Finally, the motorcycle and the trainee went straight up in the air, and over the fence, with the trainee going in one direction and the cycle in another as they landed on the outside of the fence.

"The motorcycle spun around and around until it ran out of gas, as no one could get close to it. Believe it or not, the trainee was unhurt. Needless to say, the training was broken up for that day. The sergeant looked like he was going to blow a fuse, but all the other observers were folded over in laughter. Boy, what a show!

"Finally, we received utmost training in the operation of tanks, which included the American M 4 and M 5 tanks. The M 4 was equipped with a 75mm gun, and a thirty-caliber machine gun. The M

5 was equipped with a 37mm gun, plus, two thirty-caliber machine guns. We thought the tanks were great and were quite interested in all the training, especially, the M 4 tank with the big 75mm gun.

M4 Sherman-Courtesy of Museum in Bastonge
By John Stelling.

"The tanks held five men; the tank commander, driver, assistant driver, gunner, and loader. Each one was trained in all positions. In training, it was very important to cooperate with each member of the crew. We learned a tank crew became a family in actual combat. Clyde was impressive in his skill at driving the tank from the beginning and became the best tank driver I ever saw in combat.

"At the time of this training we did not realize we would do actual battle in the greatly improved M 10, which became available to us in Africa. However, we did use the M 5 occasionally, because it was smaller and faster. We used the M 5 as bait, to draw out the German tanks, driving them crazy in battle. This training was necessary for the adventure we were destined to become a part.

"We were also trained to defend ourselves when we were out of the tank. We were later to use this training when we had taken over a town. Tank men were anxious to get out of the tank and show their skills in hand-to-hand combat. Quick action, quick thinking, and covering each other was very essential in saving lives and winning battles.

"Army training had its relaxing moments when we were allowed to take part in recreation. Games of pool, cards, dominoes, boxing, exercise equipment, and others were provided." Clyde added, "Of course Claude and I took advantage of boxing, as we thought we were pretty good. Competition between each platoon made us try a little harder to win. Many times we did win."

Claude continued, "Prior to the time when our ten weeks training was almost over, the Battalion Commander, Lt. Col. B. R. Moore, called Clyde and I, along with another set of twins, to report to his office. Commander Moore informed us that we could not serve in the same outfit. Clyde produced President Roosevelt's letter and said, "I believe you might want to read this letter." As the commander read the letter, he informed us the letter was final, and that it would be attached to our permanent record. We were never separated for the duration of World War II." The twins were never to see the letter again.

They completed their rigorous training and were given a three-day pass to return home for a final visit before going overseas. The Stokes family was told many stories about Claude and Clyde's training at Fort Knox. Mother Stokes' always liked to tell her friends about her sons on maneuvers at Fort Knox. Her favorite story was when the brothers were in their tank and Claude's head was protruding from the open turret, and Clyde was inside the tank in the driver's seat. His head was visible through the vision slit. A sergeant passed in front, calling out in astonishment: "I've gone crazy! Here's a man with two heads."

Clyde and Claude

Upon returning to Fort Knox, they were sent to Camp Campbell, Kentucky for extensive training in tank maneuvers.

Shortly after their arrival at Camp Campbell, the twins decided to see what they had at the recreation center. Claude tells this humorous incident. "We wanted to try our skills in boxing. As we entered the center, we noticed a fellow soldier punching on the punching bag. Clyde and I had won quite a few matches and were anxious to show off our skills.

"How about sparring a little with me? I asked the soldier.

"'I'll spar with you.' He replied.

"As I put on the gloves and stepped into the ring, I kept thinking I had seen this guy somewhere before this time. We both lifted up our gloves. I never got in a punch. That soldier started hitting me on the chin like he had done on the punching bag. My head was going so fast, I could hardly see. When my head stopped shaking, he asked, 'Have you had enough?' He then introduced himself as, Billy Conn. I had challenged the great prizefighter that had gone fifteen rounds with Joe Lewis. I remembered seeing his picture in the newspaper. As I look back, I can imagine Billy Conn, thinking; *I will teach this smart aleck a good lesson.* He did and I was. I have never had on another pair of boxing gloves since that day." Claude does play with this story, telling his listeners he once fought the famous Billy Conn.

Claude continued, "Camp Campbell was the last stop in our training. As we began our training, we were taken out in wooded and mountainous terrain to practice the maneuvers we had learned in our training at Fort Knox. In two weeks, we passed inspection as first class United States armored soldiers. Before we were sent to our embarkation center the Army issued us innumerable amounts of winter, wool clothing. We figured with all those clothes, we were going to an extremely cold place. We learned many times we could not out-guess the Army.

"We embarked from Newport News, Virginia on June 18, 1943, on a luxury liner that had been converted to a troop ship.

"We set sail on the Atlantic Ocean, with approximately 7,000 troops aboard, not knowing our destination. Clyde and I were fascinated with the Atlantic, as we had never seen an ocean. To us that was a big pond of water. It was beyond our imagination that a ship could be big enough to transport that many men. This was an adventure of a lifetime for us.

"About three days out, we were told we were going to Africa. That voyage was something else. Many of the troops became violently ill. Most of the men spent a greater part of their time hanging over the ship's rail or standing in line for only two meals per day. The ship had five chow stations, but with that many troops it took a long time to get fed.

"The gunners on the ship were from Oklahoma, and because we were from Oklahoma, they gave us a little tip to keep us from standing in line. They told us to volunteer for throwing over the garbage at midnight. By so doing, we could eat with the navy crew. The key to not getting sick was to keep the stomach full.

"As our ship sailed across the Atlantic, she zigzagged to keep the German submarines from getting a torpedo line-up on us. This took extra time in crossing the Atlantic because the ship had to change course every seven minutes. A great whale also followed us nearly all the way to our destination.

"After the seventh day of sailing, Clyde and I thought we would never see land again, but finally the Continent of Africa came into view. For the first time in our lives we had seen the Atlantic Ocean and a new continent. We were ready to fight for our freedom, win the war, and get back to our beloved United States of America."

-3-

World War II – Africa

The Stokes Twins arrived at the Port of Casablanca, North Africa, on June 25, 1943. They were to see for the first time a continent of many nations that had been ravaged by war. They had very little knowledge of the war in Africa that had taken place prior to their landing

The beautiful continent of Africa is the oldest civilization known to man. This civilization influenced science, literature, art, and religions of people throughout the world.

Because of African richness in natural resources of gold, diamonds, ivory, oil, and other minerals, European countries fought for a period of six hundred years as they tried to establish and control trading posts in Africa. The African colonies even fought each other for territory within the continent.

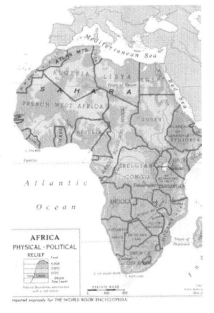

In 1884 European countries held a conference and divided Africa among themselves with only two countries remaining free, Ethiopia, and Liberia. Since that time African nations have been in constant turmoil trying to keep their territories.

World War II in Africa started in the tragic event of July 3, 1940, when the British attacked the French fleet at Mers-el-Kebir to prevent warships of their former allies from falling into enemy hands.[2]

Six times the battle swept back and forth across the rim of North Africa, but in the end, the Germans could not win because they did not control the Mediterranean. The Italian fleet was soon driven into hiding.

Marshal Rudolpho Graziani of Italy began an attack on Egypt August 6, 1940, simultaneously with an invasion of British Somaliland. He got no farther than Sidi Barrani.

The British, under Wavel, started a lightning comeback in December, which reached beyond Bengasi. But the British fell back faster in the spring when they were forced to send troops to Greece.

Again in November, 1941, the British launched an offensive, relieving Tobruk, shortly before the last Italian stronghold in Ethiopia surrendered.

Not long thereafter came Pearl Harbor, and Hitler declared war on the United States. His ultimate extirpation began to loom on the horizon then, for he had turned the spigot, which produced a flood of Allied war material and men.

There were more black days in store for the Allies, and Sunday, June 21, 1942, ranks with the blackest of them all. On that day Germany's Rommel Afrika Korps took Tobruk, aided by the Italian army, with a surprise thrust carrying him to within sixty miles of Alexandria. For a time Alexandria and Cairo were threatened, as well as the Suez Canal beyond those cities. A junction of German and Japanese forces on the shores of the Indian Ocean were also threatened. The Germans were preparing the summer offensive threatening the Soviet Union, which was to take them from Kharkov to Stalingrad. The Allies had lost Singapore, the Philippines, Burma, the Dutch East Indies, and parts of the Aleutians. Australia still was menaced, despite two Japanese air-sea defeats in the Choral Sea and at Midway in May and June.

There was a brighter spot in the allied picture when, only three weeks before, the British had carried out their first one thousand, bomber raid against Cologne. Air and tank forces from America also rushed to Africa to aid the allied forces.[3]

On October 23, 1942, the tide of battle turned against the Germans. The British Eighth Army under General Sir Bernard Montgomery, 'Monte', attacked Germany's Rommel Afrika Korps, driving the Germans back in disorderly retreat from El Alamein. This great tank victory for 'Monte' against Germany's 'Desert Fox' gave the British great encouragement as they continued pushing the German and Italian forces, reaching El Agheila on the Gulf of Sida. From there they rolled on to Tripoli, and finally, to southern Tunisia.[4]

The British advance in northwestern Africa was greatly aided by the appearance of United States forces. During the first months after the United States entered the war, American forces were unable to take a full active part in the actual fighting in Europe or Africa. America spent the first year training and building up its' troops. They did however; aid the Allies by sending bombers and troops to England to assist the 'Atlantic Fleet' in convoy operations.

On November 8, 1942, Hitler got one of the biggest surprises in his life, for a powerful American Army led by General Dwight D. Eisenhower, made a masterful surprise landing on the Mediterranean and Atlantic coasts of French North Africa.

The American forces led by General Dwight D. Eisenhower made the first large-scale appearance to begin 'Operation Torch'. These troops landed along the Atlantic coast at Morocco, and the small cities of Safi and Fidala, near Casablanca, and on the Mediterranean coast of Algeria at Oran and Algiers. A fleet of 500 merchant ships escorted by about 350 warships brought the United States forces of over 100,000, from America across the Atlantic, plus American troops from the British Isles, where they had been training for several months.

General Eisenhower made it clear to the Vichy government that the United States was at war with Germany and Italy, and not with France. He said, " We come among you to repulse the cruel invaders who would remove forever your right of self-government, your rights to religious freedom and your rights to live your own lives in peace and security." The invasion of French North Africa was a delicate matter for Eisenhower. The Allies wanted to make the invasion as completely American as possible.[5]

There was scattered resistance to the Americans, but they gained control of Algiers, Rabat and Casablanca. In only four days,

General Eisenhower, with his American forces, seized control of French North Africa on November 11, 1942. American flags were raised over the major cities of Casablanca and Algeria after Admiral Francois Darlan, commander of Vichy forces, signed a cease-fire order.

PLANNING

The allied high command plotted carefully and often—first on the north Atlantic later at

Courtesy of Associated Press

.**Planning: The allied command plotted carefully and often. First on the North Atlantic, and later at Casablanca, Ottawa, Teheran, Quebec and Yalta. This picture of the Big Three was taken at Teheran, Pictured on the front row are Stalin, President Franklin D. Roosevelt, and Winston Churchill.**

At about the same time the British, who had been engaged in a bewildering seesaw campaign on the deserts of Northern Africa for many months. Marshall Erwin Rommel and the Italians, began a combined effort eastward. General Montgomery's powerful British Army chased the 'Desert Fox' across the sands into Tunisia in a great retreat. The Americans then joined forces with the British. The Germans and Italians surrendered on May 12, 1943. It was a body blow for Hitler, rivaling the catastrophe of Stalingrad.

As the Stokes twins stepped ashore at Casablanca, Africa on June 25, 1943, they did not realize President, Franklin D. Roosevelt, had also been to Casablanca three months earlier, for a ten day council meeting. Leaders attending the council meeting were: President Roosevelt, of the United States, Prine Minister Winston Churchill of Great Britain, and General Charles de Gaulle of France.

President Roosevelt's famous words are still remembered this day as he said, "Peace can come to the world only by the total elimination of German and Japanese war power. That means the unconditional surrender of Germany, Italy, and Japan's philosophies in those countries which are based on conquest and the subjugation of other people." They decided to step up attacks on German submarines and open an all-out campaign in Sicily and Italy. [6]

As Claude and Clyde sailed into many harbors of the Mediterranean they would be going over the greatest shuttling of naval ships and equipment ever recorded in history. On November 27, Admiral de Laborde of the French high command gave orders to destroy the French Ships in the Harbor of Toulon as German troops, which then occupied most of Southern France, entered Toulon. This prevented the Germans form taking over France's greatest battle ships. The French stood by in sadness as their great Naval Fleet sank into the sea.

Claude related, "As we finally got our feet on African soil, we were met with the hot winds from the Sahara Desert. Wow, those wool army uniforms were not suitable for that hot weather. We were immediately told to report to the supply depot with our heavy barracks bags containing several sets of wool, dark green uniforms. The supply sergeant took all the contents of the bags and re-issued us only two sets of the same uniforms like we had carried over. It seems we had been used to transport new uniforms to the thousands of GIs already on the war front. We thought wrong again. No cooler clothes, for those wool uniforms were to become permanent uniforms to all soldiers on the front lines. The supply sergeant sized us up and gave us what he thought would fit. Clyde and I were pretty easy to fit as we were about 5' 8" tall and weighed one hundred forty pounds, but some of those GI's were tall and skinny and some short and heavy. Did they ever have a time, but then, we were not planning to go to a fashion show.

"We were assigned to a replacement depot in Casablanca, awaiting our final attachment to a permanent unit. While we were at this replacement center we were assigned to be guards, kitchen police, truck drivers and to perform other duties. It was not too long until Clyde and I were assigned to a convoy, transporting war supplies from

Port Casablanca to other strategic points in North Africa such as Oran, Algeria and Tunisia.

"We had a choice of vehicles all the way from a jeep to the largest truck in the Army. As those convoys were completed, each vehicle was loaded down with war materials, including food, clothing, ammunition, vehicle parts for trucks and tanks, and even airplane motors. The convoys also included the transportation of troops."

As the Twins made trips across the Sahara Desert they did not realize it was the largest desert in the world, covering approximately 3,000,000 square miles. It was almost as large as the United States. It covered most of Morocco, Algeria, Libya, Egypt, and parts of Tunisia and Sudan. From east to west across the  Sahara Desert was approximately 3,200 miles.

From June 25, 1943 to September 3, 1943 the replacement depot in Casablanca was sending large shipments of supplies to the American and Allied troops in northern Africa. Many of these supplies were eventually shipped to Sicily and then to the European Theater of War. The twins, along with thousands of other troops at the replacement depot, were most anxious to get into the big fight.

Claude mentioned, "At last we were ready to hit the road carrying needed supplies to win the war. We made several trips across that desert, sometimes traveling as many as 700 miles a trip. As we left the Port of Casablanca we could see the devastation of war as buildings lay in shambles and many, many people including children begged for food. The towns along the coast were filthy, the stench of dead bodies, and the sight of injured and dying people along the route who were covered in flies was almost too much to take. We were not allowed to stop the convoy for any reason.

"When we got away from the Atlantic coastal area, we began our possible 700 miles across the Sahara desert. Most of the Sahara was mile upon mile of hot, shifting sand dunes. You could look for miles and miles and see nothing but sand and more sand. Not a soul was in sight and we wondered how anyone could possibly live in such a desolate place. When our convoy remained still for a moment, women and little children came out of sand dunes begging for food. These hungry people literally covered our convoy in minutes. Little hungry children with sad, dirty faces were hard to refuse food when they cried out, *Hi Old Silver Away*, or cho-co-lot to the GIs. It was apparent former Americans had been there. Many of our American soldiers gave away their rations for the day to these hungry people.

"The Arab people always seemed to have money. I remember how they tried to buy food and clothing. The Arab men bought all the GI barracks bags and mattress covers they could find. They cut two holes in the bottom of the bags to put their feet through and drew the drawstring around their waist, or used the strings to make suspenders for their new pair of pants. They took the mattress covers and cut a hole out for their head and arms, making a top. Presto, a suit had been purchased and made as they had given $10.00 for the barracks bag and $20.00 for the mattress cover. The designer name was stenciled on the back of his new suit, 'USA' with the serial number of the previous owner.

"As we progressed into the trip, we didn't think we would ever see anything but sand. We changed our minds as we went through the Atlas Mountains located between Oran and Algiers. These were rugged, treacherous mountains. The roads were very narrow without any rails around the road looking down over rocky inclines where one could not see the bottom.

"Clyde and I had been accustomed to good old country cooking in Oklahoma. We were young and our stomachs took an about face as we ate the food put before us. We ate 'K' rations mostly, as we crossed Africa. A 'K' ration consisted of a can of dehydrated eggs, beef bullion for soup, a small package of crackers, and a hard chocolate candy bar. This ration was equivalent to two meals per day. We usually stayed at a fueling depot for the night where we ate from a mess hall. I can't remember what kind of food we had but I do remember we only got one slice of bread each, and it was so thin you could read through it. I suppose we got more hungry while we were serving in Africa than any other place."

Clyde remembered an experience he related, "On one of our trips I recall we had a convoy of forty vehicles carrying all the equipment and supplies we could haul. I was number forty in line when I noticed the red oil light come on. I could see I had to stop and put oil in my vehicle. I noticed several Arab men trying to hitch a ride to Algiers. As I stopped they began helping me with the problem, which caused me to return the favor by giving them a ride. By that time I was well behind the convoy and a little worried about catching up. The Arab men assured me they knew a shortcut to Algiers. Was I ever relieved when I finally caught up with the convoy? Actually, when we got to our destination I wound up being seventeen in line instead of forty. Those Arabs really knew their way across that desert and I was very grateful for their help."

Clyde was asked, "Where was your brother when you were stranded?"

"He was up front unaware I was in trouble. If you had trouble you were taught to get out of it the best way you could, and then catch up with the convoy as soon as possible."

Claude continued, "Many times as we were traveling we were strafed by gun-fire and bombed by the Germans as we carried supplies. One day I asked a soldier driving another truck where he got when our trucks were being fired upon.

" 'I got under my truck.' He explained. I looked inside his truck and he was hauling high explosives. I didn't think he had gotten in a safe place to keep from getting blown up.

"We saw a lot of things in Africa, but I believe the worst thing I viewed was when we came into the port at Oran about 7:00 a.m. one morning. There had been a big explosion on an ammunition ship killing many people on and around the ship. When we got to the dock they had pulled the ship out to sea but at least two hundred bodies had been piled up like a cord of wood. Bodies were burned beyond recognition and many had no arms or legs.

"We were told to go aboard another ship to eat breakfast. After witnessing that terrible scene I thought I could not eat breakfast, dinner, or supper. After entering the Navy mess hall where we saw all those clean cooks and smelled that food, I quickly changed my mind. We had not eaten a good meal in a month or two, and when the cooks said, 'What do you want for breakfast, and how do you want your eggs cooked?' I forgot all I had seen. I ordered six eggs with all the trimmings. That was one of the best meals I had while I was overseas.

As I think about it, it was the best meal I have ever eaten in my lifetime.

"On our last trip across the Saraha I decided I was going to be a big-shot so I chose one of the largest trucks the Army had. It was a big Diamond T that you had to use a ladder to climb into the cab. Here I was, a one hundred forty pound, skinny kid, high and lifted up. I could look down on the other GIs. They told us to pull in front of the smaller units and as I passed the other drivers, I pulled that old air horn and waved as I looked down on them. That was fun for a while but it didn't last long because I was loaded with airplane motors, which were quite heavy.

"When I got into the Atlas Mountains, I paid the price for being a show-off. I never knew what gear I had that Diamond T in since it had three-gear shift levers. As I looked over those cliffs, I thought no more big jobs for me. I had learned my lesson. I just thought I could drive anything.

" The 36th Division left New York Harbor on April 2, and landed at the Port of Oran on April 13, 1943, before we completed our last trip.[7]

"We were told to report to the bivouac area on the desert near Oran where the 636th Tank Destroyer Battalion was in training for *Operation Husky*. We were assigned to the 36th Division, and the 636th Tank Destroyer Battalion. Colonel Pyland was the commanding officer. The officers of the Battalion had access to the records of our previous training. We were lined up before the officers to be assigned to a company and then to a platoon. We were assigned to C Company, commanded by Captain Daniel Barfoot, and the Second Platoon, commanded by Lieut. Eugene Driscoll, and Staff Sgt. Glen McGuire. I remember standing before the officers as Sgt. Edward Yost who was our first tank commander of 'Jinx' said, 'I want those twins from Oklahoma.'"

The crew members serving under Sgt. Yost were: Cpl. Alvin (B. Q.) Johnson, gunner, Pfc. Joseph O'Brien, driver, Pvt. Clyde Stokes, assistant driver, and Pvt. Claude Stokes as assistant gunner. They became closely bonded to their tank buddies as they completed extensive training in preparation for their first invasion.

The Stokes twins were extremely proud to wear their 36th Division patch with a 'T' for Texas centered on an Oklahoma arrowhead of blue. The insignia was designed for the 36th Division in World War I. After the Texas National Guard was mobilized it became know as a Texas Division; however, during the World War II men

from other states were attached to the division, as replacements were needed.   Claude went on to say, "We had been trained in the Sherman

36th T Patch

M 4 and M 5 tanks back in the States, which had an enclosed turret with a 75mm gun. We

636th Tank Destroyers   were glad to see the new thirty-two ton M 10 Tiger Destroyers so called because the tank destroyer insignia is a black tiger crushing an enemy tank in its jaws. The M 10 looks much like Sherman tanks, except the long three-inch high velocity guns protrude from open turrets.   The gun had an indirect range of 14,000 yards and a direct range of about 2,000 yards. Clyde and I were really impressed.

"The M 10 tank destroyers were powered by diesel engines and the M4 and M 5 Sherman tanks were powered by gasoline engines. We preferred the diesel engine of the M 10.

"We were most anxious to learn the operation of the new M 10 Tank. Training was very extensive as Lt. Col. John W. Casey of Chicago, Illinois furnished textbook material to all our commanders on the versatile use of anti-tank weapons when there were no tanks to fight."

Claude and Clyde learned through this training that concepts in the use of tank destroyers had been radically changed. Originally they were regarded as a special purpose, semi-independent force whose sole duties were to engage enemy tanks in combat. The M 10 was used, not only, in defensive roles but also for general division reconnaissance and for direct support of the infantry.

Claude related,   "The bivouac where we were housed consisted of lines of tents on the desert. Food was hard to come by in Africa. We survived mostly on K or C Rations, but we occasionally got something else to eat. Sometimes men obtained a pass to go into a nearby town where they were able to purchase food and share with others. This didn't happen very often. The officers in the Battalion seemed to eat a little better than the other troops.

"I recall a funny incident that happened while we were located at this bivouac. One of the guys in our platoon found out the officers had some steak, so he sneaked out and cut a hole in the mess tent where the steak was located. He came back to our platoon and got out his gasoline issued stove and preceded to cook the steak.

"On that still, dry desert you could smell food cooking for miles. The officers missed their steak and sniffed their way to our tent. As Jones was hovering over his delicious steak, making sure it was cooked just right, two officers peeked over his shoulder and one said, 'Jones do you like steak?' "

"Jones responded in his long Texas drawl, 'yeees Surrrh, if you put a little bit of white gravy with it.' The officers grinned and walked away leaving Jones to enjoy his steak.

"While we were on location in the desert, a German pilot came for a visit every day at 12:00 o'clock noon and put on a big show. He did all kinds of acrobatics as he dived and rolled over cutting all sorts of de doe's. He tantalized our American pilots into going up to chase him. When they went up, he took off and they could not catch him because his German plane was lighter and faster.

"Someone came up with the idea to strip a P38 fighter plane down with nothing but two machine guns. The American pilot went up before noon and flew high above where the German plane could not see him. Sure enough, here came old 'Fritz', rolling and putting on his big show. Then, out of nowhere came our P 38 and the race was on. To the German's surprise the American P38 caught up to him and shot him down.

"All of us on the ground cheered as old 'Fritz' hit the sand with his last show. The American pilot proceeded to put us on a good show himself as we all cheered."

On September 3, 1943 the Stokes twins boarded a ship at the Port of Oran with their 36th Division, and sailed up the coast of Northwest Africa to arrive at the Port of Biserte in extreme North Africa on September 6, 1943. They embarked for this port to take part in their first invasion of Europe. The time had come when they were to defend their United States of America by portraying their allegiance, standing in battle to defend the people they loved.[8]

-4-

World War II – Invasion of Italy

Allied Timetable in Italy

Fifth Army
Patch

The Stokes Twins were on their way to their first invasion as they embarked from the Port of Bizarte in North Africa on September 6, 1943, on a British ship. Soon after leaving the harbor, they were informed the 36th Division was headed for Salerno, Italy.[1]

In early July 1943, General Dwight D. Eisenhower's army, brilliantly supported by the combined fleets and superior air power of the Allies, invaded Sicily off the toe of the Italian boot.

The Allied lightning-war outmatched Hitler's efforts in the first days of the conflict. Allied planes bombarded Sicily for over a week starting on July 10, 1943, allowing General George C. Patton and his American troops to plunge forward to Palermo where the German army had fled. The Italian army surrendered at Palermo on July 23, 1943.[2]

Mussolini saw Hitler and pleaded for aid. Instead, Hitler advised Mussolini to abandon southern and central Italy and stand on the river Po. On the day of their last meeting, military objectives in Rome were heavily bombarded by a predominately American air force and the Italian people were in a panic.

On July 25, 1943, Mussolini resigned. His regime was over. King Victor Emmanuel named Marshal Badoglio to succeed him. One arm of the Axis had been severed.

General Patton, who was very aggressive, continued to march across Sicily arriving in Messina shortly before Field Marshall Montgomery and his British troops. Patton's troops overpowered the Germans and Italians capturing approximately 130,000 prisoners. The conquest of Sicily took only 38 days when the Italians surrendered on August 17, 1943.

The American 45th Division took part in the Sicily invasion. Staff Sgt. Carl Stokes, the twins' older brother was an infantryman in the 45th Division, along with two close personal friends today, Howard J. D. Tolson, and Edward E. Gene Weeks.

Claude related, "We thought we would get some good food on the British ship similar to the chow we had gotten on American ships as the American Navy really fed us well. We were wrong again. When our troops went aboard that British ship, our American food was to accompany us but we discovered the British kept our food and fed us their British rations which consisted of bully beef, a hard tack, and tea, pronounced t-a-y. The hard tack was similar to a biscuit that had been cooked for a month and put in the air. Only the *Good Lord* knew how long those things had been stored on that British ship. I remember Lt. Driscoll challenged the officer in charge of the mess hall when he said, 'these biscuits have weevils in them.' "

"The British officer replied. 'Don't you bloody *Yanks* know what caraway seeds are?' "

"'That is the first time I ever saw a caraway seed crawl.' Lt. Driscoll retorted.' "

"Well, you get a bunch of hungry GIs together and they will come up with a solution for most any problem. We got an ax from the firebox and chopped an opening in a wooden wall going down into the 'hole' where the American food was being stored. With our luck, the only thing we could reach was graham crackers. To this day I am not very fond of graham crackers after eating them for three days on that ship.

Clyde added, "On a ship there is not a lot of things to do, but sleep and eat. Most GIs passed their time playing black jack, poker, or dice. Claude and I did not take part in their games but watched from the sidelines. We were paid $50.00 per month and we were not going to take a chance on losing our money. We watched with others as one black GI and one white GI were competing for most all the money they had won on the ship. I remember men were standing all around them; some who had money left were making side bets. The black GI was sweating so much he had to have a towel man to mop his brow. I can't remember who won the money."

Claude's last memory concerning the British ship came as they had been on the beach of Salerno for a few hours. He said, "We looked out to see the old British ship pull out to sea, when a German dive bomber put a bomb right down the smoke stack of the ship. I could not help thinking that those crawling caraway seeds were all gone.

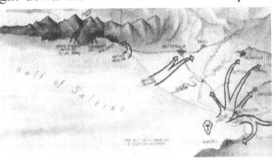

Beachhead of Salerno

General Mark Clark's American 5th Army landed at Salerno, Italy, on September 9, 1943. Claude continues his memoirs concerning their first landing as he relates, "We were a little leery of all the pep talk we had been given while we were still aboard the ship. We knew the Italians had surrendered and were told we would be marching down the streets of Salerno, pronto. Wrong again.[3]

"The 36th Division, under the command of Major General Fred L. Walker, landed at 3:30 a. m. on September 9, 1943. The 36th Division was the first American division to invade the European mainland. Our 636th Tank Destroyer Battalion troops went ashore on September 10, while our tanks were being unloaded from LSTs. There was no doubt in our minds that the Germans knew we were landing at Salerno. They were dug in, heavily fortified with artillery, mortars, machine guns, armored tanks, and an overpowering German air support. It took a while to get our tanks and crews together up and down the beachhead but little by little we fought with the infantry until we connected with our company and tank, and when we did, things started clicking."

Clyde added, "By the time we got organized with our tanks and got ready for battle, the Germans had overrun our infantry, cutting off some from our 36th Division. For three days the battle for position went back and forth. We gained ground only to lose it again."

Claude remarked, "As I look back remembering the state of confusion we were in, knowing we were facing great odds with green troops on our first invasion and fighting the Germans who were well experienced, I have come to this conclusion: *God* was truly on our side. Clyde and I were not Christians at the time and did not give God credit for the great victory that was to be ours then, but we do know now that no human beings could have pulled off such a victory without God. Our parents were surely praying for us back in the States. I am sure there were many prayers going up for our troops in that day and time. That is the only way I can explain the miracle of coming out of that battle alive.

Salerno Beach Party

"Things looked pretty grim as we heard old *Axis Sally* announce on her radio program that our Fifth Army was in great peril as the Germans were advancing against Allied Forces and pushing us back into the sea. The British also reported that Allied Forces were near collapse all across the Salerno beachhead. We didn't need to hear all that stuff as we could see our infantry was taking a beating all along the beachhead.

"The infantry fought against great odds, digging fox holes, trying to hold their position despite the German's overpowering artillery and infantry power. Casualties were high with no replacements coming in, but our troops were determined to hold their positions and start advancing instead of retreating. We meant business and we were going to take that beachhead despite the odds.

"On Sept. 13 and 14, the real test came when the Germans were attacking in full force, rolling out their big Mark 4 and Mark 5 Tanks, equipped with 88mm guns

An infantry officer

that had a much higher velocity than our three-inch 50mm gun on our M 10. Not only did they have bigger tanks, their infantry and artillery barrage heavily supported their attacks. We were given a section of the beach to protect and hold which was the very place the Germans chose to attack.[4]

"The enemy pounded us all night on September 13. The following day they made their attack with thirteen tanks as they headed our way. I recall a general coming by and saying, 'No man leaves this hill unless he is carried off on a stretcher.' And about in the same breath he said, 'Here they come men! If you can't swim to Sicily, or if you don't like sauerkraut and wieners, you had better stop those Germans, now!'

"Those orders put C Company into action. I don't know about the rest of our unit, but Clyde and I didn't think we could swim that distance, and we sure didn't like sauerkraut.

"We were dug in right behind the infantry. It was a classic example of using the tank destroyer in close support of the infantry and it bucked up the morale of our troops to see our big M10 tank destroyers supporting them.

"While artillery blasted at the enemy from the beaches, the tank destroyers were firing at them from both flanks. The enemy was caught in a terrific crossfire.

"Our Jinx M 10 tank, commanded by Sgt. Edwin Yost, went into full action, knocking out five Mark 4 German tanks, one ammunition truck, one armored half-track, and one pill box. We also captured a house harboring Germans and overpowered them, capturing around 180 of they're infantrymen. This action broke up and stopped the enemy attack and saved the beachhead at Salerno. (As a general told us)

"We can tell you those huge German tanks scared us plenty in the beginning. Even though their fire power velocity was greater than the American M 10, we learned to out- maneuver the Germans as we noticed our tanks were faster when it came to aiming and getting off the first shots before they could get their 88mm guns focused. In a real tank battle we didn't wait like sitting ducks, we got right up in their midst and let them have it with all our quick maneuvering which resulted in knocking out their tanks first."

For this gallantry in action Clyde and Claude were awarded the *Silver Stars*, (picture below left to right) with Staff Sgt. Raymond G. Murphy of Jacksonville, Florida, Sgt. Edwin A. Yost of Gorham, Kansas, Cpl. Alvin B. Q. Johnston of Snyder, Texas, Pfc. Joseph O'Bryan of New Haven, Kentucky, and Privates Claude and Clyde Stokes of McAlester, Oklahoma.

We were amused to see the picture of their receiving the Silver Stars. The caption on this famous picture had the names in reverse as Clyde is on the extreme right.) In books and news articles their names were reversed 90% of the time.

Claude chuckled, "We never dreamed we would get medals for all that fighting. It only took us twenty-five minutes. You talk about teamwork, that crew on Jinx had it? Everyone did his own job and did it with skill and accuracy.

"The Germans were not through trying to push us back. The 636th Tank Destroyer Battalion was assigned a 1500-yard sector to protect and defend in the vicinity of La Cosa Creek and the Calore River located behind the Sele River. This was a strategic crossing and the battalion went into action as the Germans launched two hostile air attacks followed by a heavy armored attack. Some of the enemy tanks succeeded in crossing La Cosa Creek, overrunning the positions held by the battalion's reconnaissance company. Our battalion went in with all we had, holding this emergency outpost, with members of the unit firing machine guns and rifles point blank into the approaching tanks and engaging the enemy vehicles with hand grenades. Our tanks delivered almost constant fire from our three-inch tank destroyer guns into the mighty enemy armor.

"Even though the enemy supported its attack with heavy artillery concentration supported by their superior 88mm gun, our 636th Tank Destroyer Battalion prevented a breakthrough which would have threatened the solidarity of the entire beachhead. Because of this outstanding performance of duty in action, the *Fighting 636th* was awarded *The Presidential Unit Citation*."

Clyde added, "The Navy moved in and pounded the German positions with big naval guns and the 82nd Airborne brought their C 47s pushing the Germans out for good.

"By that time we were getting assistance in the invasion up and down the beachhead of Salerno as the 45th Division, the 445th T. D. Battalion, the 601st T. D. Battalion, the 82nd Airborne Division, and the 75lst Tank Battalion made their presence known. I must say, there was not another infantry division in World War II that fought against such great odds and still came through victoriously as did the 36th Division."

"And that's no brag, just facts," Claude added.

Some of the many Salerno heroes can be found by logging on to the web site of the 36th Division, World War II Memorial in Austin, Texas, and by scanning the Salerno heroes. One can read the accounts of men like Sgt. Charles E. Kelley, the first to be decorated with *The Congressional Medal of Honor* for action on the European Continent. Also included are Sgt. James Logan, Pvt. William A. Crawford, and 1st Lt. Arnold J. Bjorkland, and S/Sgt. Manuel "Ugly" Gonzales, who was noted to be the finest in his company, netting him *The Distinguished Service Cross*.

Claude continued with much feeling. "As we view these recorded heroes, we are reminded of the many heroes who died on the Salerno Beachhead who have never been recognized. Out of the over 50,000 troops of the American Fifth Army fighting, no record that we can find, has been recorded as to how many casualties of brave men washed up on the shores of Salerno. Nor how many died in the most frantic battle we ever encountered. Courageous men died trying to hold on to the beachhead, advancing inch by inch under tremendous odds.

"We cannot begin to explain what emotion we feel today as we look back and recall the scene of those dying on the Salerno Beachhead who literally paved the way for victory to come to Allied forces. All men who stepped from landing crafts into the blue waters of the Tyrrhenian Sea, and waded ashore at Salerno are our heroes. Not only infantrymen, but medics, artillery, signal, ordnance, and quartermaster men, reconnaissance troops, and headquarters personnel. Those who fought so gallantly and died that we might live. As we look back over the last fifty-six years and remember the publicity Clyde and I have been given, we pause and bow our heads in shame for those who were not recognized as the true American Heroes.

Claude and Clyde in Parade, photo-1993

"The 36th Division continued from Salerno, going up the boot of Italy from town to town. Close calls were routine in the month of September, 1943. Clyde and I were on guard duty one night with our M 10 tank, Jinx, parked behind a little ridge. We got out of the tank and dug our fox holes about fifty feet apart, thinking we could do our guard duty and be somewhat protected. Just as we got settled, a German bomber came over and dropped a bomb right between us, covering us with dirt and rocks. Neither of us was hit but it didn't do much for our eardrums. I think that is the reason I say 'huh' so much to my wife today.

"Well the good part of the story is that our anti aircraft guns shot the bomber down and the crew bailed out with one falling in our sector. All who bailed out were captured. The one we captured was the tail gunner, but to our surprise she was a woman. I don't know, but this could be the only woman tail gunner captured in World War II. How lucky can you get?

"Things began to get a little better along about September 20. Company C was assigned to security for the Fifth Army Headquarters and the rest of the battalion was put in reserve for the rest of September.

"On September 23, 1943, Clyde and I realized the 45thDivision was fighting in the sector, when we recognized some of the Company K men who were friends of our older brother, Carl. We started trying to find Carl, but we only saw three of his buddies from McAlester: Dodge Dickens, Schilcht Billy, and Ralph Hall. Each told us they had seen Carl just a few minutes before. We never made connections with Carl and later learned from our parents that Carl had been wounded on September 23. We were halfway across the world and missed seeing our brother by about twenty minutes.

"The month of October, 1943, was a little better than September; however, there is never good times in war. We still faced the same dangers as we dodged rifle bullets, shrapnel from shells, bombs falling, mines planted by the Germans, plus many other hazards of war. Great danger of being killed was not confined to the Salerno Beachhead, as shells played no favorites. The new replacement troops coming in were very vulnerable as they came on the battlegrounds as nervous, scared, and inexperienced men. Some matured into real soldiers in only a few hours. For some it took longer. Some never made it.

"After our American Fifth Army secured Salerno, we had the Germans on retreat as we captured cities and towns like, Altavilla, Paestum, and Capaccio on our continued march up the boot of Italy.

"We advanced toward Naples with the Germans on the defensive. We wanted to forget the hardships suffered at Salerno, La Cosa Creek and the Calorie River, plus all the cities and towns we had conquered between Salerno and Naples.

Claude, Cpl. Rosecoe G. Russel
Clyde, Naples, Italy

"On October 1,1943, American troops captured Naples and the city of Avillino. As the 36th Division headed into Naples, we were carrying ammunition to the American 82nd Airborne paratroopers who had been reported as having run out of ammunition. When we arrived, the German army had withdrawn.

"Naples with a city of over a million people lay in ruins as the Germans destroyed tons of Italian ships in the harbor.

The 82nd Airborne had been quite busy, as they had already set up restaurants and places of entertainment and recreation. Some of the places we shall not mention.

"I remember we sought out an old castle in Naples where the Fifth Army would house their headquarters. Wow! This old country boy never had seen a place like that. I remember the high ceilings, draped windows, and beautiful art hanging on the walls. The things that I remember with delight were the many bedrooms in that old castle. As we entered the rooms we saw big, tall, four-poster beds with feather mattresses and clean white sheets. I remember Clyde saying, 'Man we just made it to heaven.' After sleeping on a steel cramped tank floor for months it was *Heaven*. The Italian ladies who kept and cleaned the rooms got beside themselves when they came in and saw nasty, dirty, unshaven GIs clad in muddy boots and clothes lying right up in the middle of those fine white beds. We heard exclamations of *Mama Mia* all over the place, but it would have taken more than *Mama Mia* from a cleaning lady to get us off those beds.   Well,   so   much   for Heaven.

"Our   little   rest   didn't last   long,   but   we   heard   of Caserta Rest Camp which was located a few miles from Naples where some of our troops got a real tank; however, old tank men had to keep on the move."

"On   the   last   day   of October,   in   a   town   beyond Naples,   our   2nd   Platoon   of Company C was placed on

Caserta Rest Camp

detachment service with the anti tank regiment of the British 7th Armored Division. We were assigned to train the British in the operation of our American M 10 tank destroyer. This was quite an experience. The British were different than Americans. They never got in a hurry for anything. It didn't matter if you were driving a tank or shooting at Germans, when 2 and 4 o'clock came they dropped everything to have their tea. We spent more time going to tea than we did teaching them the operation of the M 10 tank. Their menu was that old bully beef, hard tack, and tea. 'Yuck'! I won't drink tea to this day.[6]

"A day never went by that we didn't get cursing and Mama Mia from property owners as those British drivers cut wide grooves across the front of nearly every house in their town. The M 10 tank was about eight feet across and had a sharp knife-like edge protruding which left its brand on each house as the British went down their narrow streets. Clyde was teaching the British to drive and he failed that task. As we left their little town those Italians were waving hands and speaking fast Italian language we couldn't understand.

"The first week in November our C Company returned to the 636th tank unit and we were plenty glad to be reunited with Company A and B. We were even happy to eat our C rations again instead of that bully beef and tea.

"The month of November brought on more enemies for the American troops in Italy. The Italian fall rains became one of our worst nightmares as it rained and rained and rained for as many as seventeen straight days without ceasing. The constant movement of German and American troops made a muddy, boggy mess in a war-torn country. Vehicles bogged down to the floorboards, having to be pulled out by wench trucks. Convoys of replacements and supplies were stalled in mud for hours, sometimes being caught out in the open by heavy fire from the Germans.

"Infantrymen had a difficult time as they slipped and sloshed through knee-deep, slick, slimy mud which pulled the best part of their energy from them. We thought we tank men had it better. At least we didn't have to walk in the mud and rain or sleep in pup tents covering a dug trench half full of water.

"The enemies of fatigue, hunger, misery, and loneliness for home were ever present with the fighting GIs. Axis Sally didn't help any, as she did her radio broadcasts, playing on the emotions of our men. I have seen soldiers go berserk when she said, 'You American GIs don't worry about your wives and girl friends for they are having a good time with those garrison soldiers back in the States.'

"Another enemy was the mountain terrain our tanks had to climb, never knowing what was just around the curves of those narrow circling roads. One tank in our platoon slid over the edge of the mountain going end over end. The Germans had ample time to get well positioned on the high cliffs of the mountains. They had the greater advantage as they looked down on American troops, giving them perfect observation points, covering all roads, small towns, and villages.

"Our 636th Tank Destroyers were not much help to the infantry in mountainous territory as we only fired direct fire when the infantry forward observer called for fire on a certain target which was in our view. We also did indirect firing on targets we could not see, miles away. Actually, we were firing artillery day and night. We got very little sleep because the Germans could see the muzzle flash from our guns at night and would call fire down on us in return.

"We had our 'Jinx' tank dug in behind a little knoll where the German's 88 mm gun could not get us. They were perched so high their guns could not be lowered to a position to hit our tank. These made the shells zoom about four feet over our heads, which would almost suck us out of the tank. We finally realized they could not hit us because of their gun position, but those 'zoom', 'zoom' shells going over our tank played havoc with our nerves and our ears. We lost numerous men due to stress resulting in our getting new replacements.

"A tank was very confining and the noise was tremendous. Many could not face death at such an early time in their lives. We lost numerous tanks and men in the lull of movement as it took us days to travel twenty-five miles.

"I recall getting a replacement in our tank, who was not conditioned to the shells going over the tank in the 'zoom' fashion. Somehow, we had been given slices of bread to eat with our rations. As we sat on the bottom of the steel tank floor eating bread and jelly, the shells started firing over us. As I looked over at the replacement, I noticed he had squeezed the bread and jelly until it was running through his fingers like mush. I thought to myself, this poor guy is scared to death. I was really convinced he was scared as I felt a warm substance run under me. He eventually could not take the pressure and was transferred to the medics. Some could not take the pressures that were placed upon them.

"Being confined in the tank was no picnic for our crew, but we became more conditioned battle after battle. Helping to save lives of infantrymen far outweighed our discomforts. The M 10 tank was confining, it was true, but the old warrior weighed thirty-two tons and gave us a degree of protection. Inside the tank we had about eight feet, including the central control mechanism, located in the center of the tank. Two men could curl up around the control and sleep on the steel tank floor. The gunner and driver slept while sitting up in their chairs, which tilted to some degree. There was also one other chair that could be raised up or down from the sides when sitting became possible.

"The infantry ousted the enemy from those mountain caves and enclosed cliffs by using hand grenades, machine guns, and small arms as they struggled up the rugged mountains with the Germans looking right down their throats.

"On November 25, 1943 our Battalion Commander came by and said, 'Every man in this man's army is going to get a hot meal on Thanksgiving with all the trimmings.'

On Million Dollar Mountain

"Boy! That was good news for us. We could hardly wait as the cooks set up tarp tents and cooked the dinner. We really didn't know how we could get off the front lines, leave our tanks, and quit firing on the Germans long enough to eat that hot meal. We faced getting killed, but we thought it was worth the try. "It was raining so hard we could not see the tank next to ours. The temperature hovered near freezing as we made our way to the cook's covered tarp to area; we wound up with turkey soup topped with slushy pumpkin pie. There was no way we could keep the rain out...Oh well, we had to give the cooks and 'A' as they tried to cook us a hot meal.

"The remainder of the month of November was more of the same shelling, same rain, cold, and mud. We lost several tanks and many men were wounded or killed. Again, Clyde and I escaped injury.

"Late November and early December of 1943 found us trying to withstand the Germans through the Italian rains and snow storms,

making our troops wet to the bone and shivering from the cold. It seemed the mountains were endless as we crept along the treacherous territory. Mt. Maggiore stands out vividly in my memory.

Million Dollar Mountain

" This mountain was known as the *Million Dollar Mountain*, where over six hundred Allied guns fired at the mountain in one night. One hundred planes bombed and strafed the old mountain day and night, costing over a million dollars in ammunition and equipment, not to mention the men who gave their lives. [7]

"Then came the mountains of Mount Sombrero and Mount Lungo. The cities of San Pietro, San Vittore, Venafro, and Highway Six which had to be taken before we could enter the Liri Valley."

Clyde said, "Taking San Pietro was very costly for our tank destroyers. We went down the road to San Pietro with sixteen tanks and returned with four. One of those returning tanks was our Jinx."

Claude went on to say with sorrow in his voice, "War is a terrible tragedy in the lives of all involved. Scenes were etched in our memory as we captured mountain after mountain and town after town. We remember the town of San Pietro so vividly. Because of the constant battling of Germans and Americans taking and retaking this city. It became a pitiful sight as it was reduced to rubble and piles of stones.

"The saddest thing to see was the pain on faces of the families who had left their homes for safety and returned with nothing left but a pile of stone and perhaps, a sign or family marker. They were left without food, clothing, or a dry place to stay. The hopelessness of the situation, caused by continuous war, left them in a state of despair. Joy could not come to the soldiers who conquered these people. The only joy we could see was that we were leaving them with a better hope for the future."

Claude continued with his farmer boy story about mules, "The infantry had to use mules to transport rations and ammunition up those steep mountains and then bring back the wounded and dead on their return. This scene was too horrible and heartbreaking to describe. Even the mules became shell-shocked. As a shell exploded near one of those mules, he would go crazy and become hard to handle. The Italian soldiers were supposed to handle the mules but they were in worse shape than the mules, especially as they tried to dodge all the German booby traps and mines. The lot finally fell upon the American troops to take control of the mules.

Pack Mules

"In a Texas unit, you would think it would be easy to find muleskinners, but it wasn't. No one wanted to admit they knew how to do such a lowly job. Not only were the mules completely worn out from their heavy burdens but they didn't seem to understand English, only the Italian.

"In the month of December the German Air Force turned out daily to bomb and strafe our positions. The Germans had a habit of doing the same thing each day, day after day. After two days of this air maneuvering of a pilot around Mount Lungo, we finally got his pattern. He was flying so low we could see the scarf around his neck. The third day, I was waiting for him. Our tank had a 50 caliber machine gun on top of the turret. I lined the gun up where he had been coming, and sure enough, here he came. I pulled the trigger and held it. Old 'Fritzy Boy' ran right into my line of fire and down he came. No fancy shooting just knew where to shoot. Another C Company tank got another plane on the same day. That stopped the bombing and strafing for a while.

"I recall an incident involving an Italian soldier while we were dodging the strafing. As I heard a German plane going over us, I saw an Italian outside our tank jumping up and down with glee as he said, '*Americano, Americano.*' " I said, "No, no, *Tedesco* (German). About that time the German dropped a bomb covering the little Italian in dirt and rocks.

"He pulled himself out of the debris saying, '*Mama Mia, Mama Mia,*' " as he brushed himself off.

"The last week in December our tanks supported the infantry in taking the town of Unefro, and Hill 730. Then came Christmas, which was a sad time for all GI's. For the first time in our lives, Clyde and I were away from our beloved home during Thanksgiving and Christmas. We sure did miss the good food and fellowship with the Stokes family back on the farm in Oklahoma. We did get a Christmas present though, by getting relieved off the front line on Christmas. We went on bivouac near a little town, spending our time servicing equipment, getting accustomed to new replacements, and training and organizing our crews.

"Being relieved from the front lines was a treat we looked forward to. First, we weren't being shot at all the time. Second, we got baths and clean clothes. The sergeant issued us clean clothing and replaced any worn-out or lost items. At this particular time, it seemed half of Company C had lost their wool knit caps we wore under our helmets in the wintertime. The Italians liked the caps because they were warm and could be washed. The supply sergeant was upset because he had run out of the caps and was going to make us pay for replacements. Lt. Driscoll said to me, 'Get a jeep, we are going to town.'

"After we reached town, I noticed about half of the people on the street were wearing Army knit wool caps. As I drove down the street slowly, Lt. Driscoll stepped out of the jeep and grabbed the caps from all those Italians. It didn't take us long until we had collected enough caps for the whole company. I was glad to get off the street, because as we left, those Italians were hollering and shaking their fists at us. I was glad I didn't understand what they were saying. I had a good idea they were telling us they had bartered with our GIs for those caps. You can be assured they were not inviting us to Sunday school and Church.

"The 36th Division had taken a beating in the four previous months. Our 636th Tank Destroyer Battalion received many replacements as casualties ran very high. Company C was no exception. We lost Sgt. Yost, our tank commander, who was wounded. Cpl. Russell took his position for a very short time and was sent back to his former position. The old tank destroyer, Jinx went into the rest area as a hero, with six silver stars, numerous purple hearts, The Presidential Unit Citation, ten German tanks destroyed, and one airplane."

On January 17, 1944, the twin's battered old tank destroyer came out of the bivouac rest area, not as the Jinx, but as the 'Oklahoma Wildcat'. She had a new name, a new tank commander, Sgt. Claude H. Stokes, a new driver, Sgt. T 4, Clyde T. Stokes, and a new gunner, Cpl. Daniel S. Sklar.

"I can't remember who the extra gunner was," Claude said, " We had so many replacements at that time. Some lasted only a short time and then we were given others. I do recall Cpl. Joseph O'Bryan and T5, B. Q. Johnston were promoted to sergeants; therefore becoming commanders of other tanks within the platoon.

"We were proud of the old battered 'Oklahoma Wildcat' as she pulled out with her new name painted on both sides and on the front. Many laughed at her new name, especially foreigners. They didn't know 'Okies' could tame a wildcat in no time. She became our best friend throughout Italy, France and Germany.

The Oklahoma Wildcat

"The battered old gal wound up with wounds, blown tracks, damaged motors, and many other less-serious injuries. She was much like us today. She showed her age and what she had been through, as she continued to be the fastest tank in the 636th Tank Destroyer Battalion."

Claude and Clyde recalled many stories to tell their families about their service time. They could not always remember the exact place or time, but could recall many of the incidents.

Claude chuckled, "In January, 1944, we were suppose to attack a small town early one morning. Customarily, when our battalion could not see movement in a town, we sent a patrol out to scout the area and determine whether or not we would have to shoot up the town. Sometimes the Germans were gone but many times we had to flush them out. I recall when Sgt. Glen McGuire, our platoon sergeant, two other men, and I went out to scout the town. We crawled up a little creek bed to the road leading to a bridge that crossed over the road. Dawn was just breaking as we crawled under the bridge and reached the other side.

"We suddenly came face to face with a little fat, Italian man about five feet tall. He was dressed in a tuxedo, a tall black silk hat, and carried a big key he had made from cardboard. He seemed to know our purpose for being under his bridge was to scout the area.

" 'Mayor of city,' he announced. 'Tedesco (Germans) left.' He quickly handed Sgt. McGuire his big key to the city, and suddenly grabbed old McGuire and started kissing him. He turned to me and proceeded to kiss me. Then he turned back to McGuire and kissed him once, but by that time McGuire didn't want anymore of his kisses. He pulled his pistol and said, 'If that little … kisses me one more time, I'm going to shoot him.' "

"It was hard to constrain McGuire, but we managed to get on with our business and let the dressed-up little dude do the same.

"Another incident occurred in one of those Italian towns I will never forget. When we were relieved off the front lines, we always sought home-cooked food. There were no restaurants, of course, but the Italians opened up their homes and cooked meals for us. In Italy, tame rabbit was their main source of meat. Several men in our platoon had eaten at this particular house the day before so we were most anxious to get reservations again.

"When we knocked on the door, a little girl said, 'Papa is out back preparing meat for a meal to feed the soldiers.' Well, we went out back and found Papa. He wasn't skinning tame rabbits but a big fat tomcat. Hides of previous cats were attached to a clothesline. We knew then, what we had eaten the day before. I'm not going to say what Sgt. McGuire called Papa, as this is not an 'X' rated book. I think if I had not gotten the sergeant out of there, plenty pronto, Papa would not have shown up for dinner that night.

"The last of January, we attempted to cross the Rapedo River. We had to cross this same river many times as it ran around through the mountains, but this encounter with the German tanks and infantry, was to be the most costly in the loss of lives.

"The Germans had every inch covered with heavy mortar, machine guns, artillery fire, and what we called the 'Screaming Memie' gun, which had a six barrel mortar, called Nebelwerfer.

"Old Screaming Memie had the grinding, roaring sound somewhat like a huge motor having difficulty starting, combined with the sound of hundreds of large-winged birds fluttering right overhead. That loud whirling sound would scare the pants right off anyone in its pathway. When we heard that familiar Memie coming we realized it would explode six different rounds in a radius of about seventy-feet. If we were not in a tank, we headed for the nearest foxhole.

"No one was exempted from danger of the German firepower as we crossed the river. At this particular point of crossing, it probably measured one hundred feet across. We, as well as the Germans, were dug in and returning fire across the river. We fired our 3/50mm gun so long and fast that the barrel got so hot it would not go back into recoil preventing it from firing. Clyde was driving the 'Oklahoma Wildcat' like a seasoned pro, which he surely was. Cpl. Daniel Sklar, the gunner, was pouring on the shots as directed, and I might add, with great skill. As commander of the Oklahoma Wildcat, I waited until the German firepower slowed down and took a bucket, running to the river, and carried water to cool off the gun barrel. On one of these trips, I didn't make it back to the tank before the shelling started again.

" I jumped into the slit trench I had dug just for this kind of emergency. As I lay face down for protection, I heard a frying, sizzling sound in the mud nearby. As I turned my head, I saw the nose of an 8-inch artillery shell, sticking in the muddy bank of my slit trench, about six inches from my head. I reasoned; since the shell did not explode on impact, I had about fifteen seconds to make a most important decision. I could jump out of the trench, which would give me a 95% chance of getting wounded or killed by steel fragments from the shell, or machine gun fire from the enemy. If I stayed in the trench, I could take my chance of the shell being a dud. This did happen at times, as the Polish were known for sabotaging ammunition in German ammunition plants. The Germans made their captives work on assembly lines, supplying them needed materials to fight the war. Today, I thank some Polish person for making that dud.

"As I look back to that time of danger and read my Holy Bible, I am reminded of the story of Moses as he was trying to lead the Israelites from bondage in Egypt. God sent ten plagues on Pharaoh and the Egyptians. One of those ten plagues was God turning all rivers and streams into blood. The Rapedo River was just that. When I dipped my bucket into the river, it was red from blood. Many brave men had fallen in crossing, but God had spared our lives again. Infantrymen had repeatedly tried to wade or swim across the river being caught by German fire.

"War was a terrible thing, but we endured the horrors, by being so busy trying to stay alive, that there was no time to think. We tried to think of home to replace the horror of seeing death on the faces of men. We carried a greater burden, knowing we had taken lives. We had been taught in our training that it was kill or be killed. Many GIs could not handle this burden of guilt. To replace the image of men dying, we tried to think of home, which made us more determined to advance on the enemy and bring the horrible war to a victorious end.

"Our tank destroyers could not cross until the engineers were able to construct a pontoon bridge across the Rapedo River. They paid a great price with lives lost as they constructed bridges under heavy fire while we did our best to protect them. They are seldom mentioned, but they played an integral part many, many times as they cleared areas and built bridges across numerous rivers, allowing American troops to pursue the enemy."

Clyde added, "We finally did cross the river, paying a terrible price on both sides. The 36th Division lost 1600 men in one night. A truce was called to pick up the dead and wounded American and German soldiers. It seemed to us that the 36th Division and the 636th Tank Destroyer Battalion got more than our share of this kind of assignments."[8]

Claude went on to say, "During the month of February, 1944, the miserable conditions of snow, sleet, constant rain, and muddy weather continued to prevail. As Clyde drove the Oklahoma Wildcat through all that mud, we could not help remember our growing up on the farm with our sisters, La Vern and Eupalee. They could have had a field day with all that mud to make mud pies as they played 'house'. Just another thought of home.

"Occasionally our mail caught up with us. GIs looked forward to mail call. Any word from home was sweet music to us. Our sister, La Vern wrote to us almost everyday, keeping us up on all the news about the rest of the family. Many friends wrote to us and some, of whom we had never met.

November Rain and Mud

Two of those friends were Frances Anderson and Dorene Goatcher, who lived on adjacent farms in the Mitchell community where we farmed most of our lives. Our girl friends, Betty and Madlyn had moved to California, where their parents worked in the shipyards for the war effort, but the girls were still writing, praying, and waiting for us. We saw many GIs get *Dear John Letters*, while some were elated to get pictures of their babies they had never seen. Occasionally, we had time to write, but not very long at a time. We were not allowed to give out any information on where we were, or what we were doing, as our mail was strictly censored.

"As we continued to creep along through the sticky mud, we were wet to the bone and miserably cold. Severe cold weather in Italy had reached an all time high for us, as the blinding snow and sleet made traveling most miserable.

"At times during all this misery, we had the opportunity to get a little rest outside the cramped tank quarters. We were told the best place for getting warm was in a cowshed, where the cow manure would produce heat and warm our bodies. Some tank crews didn't go for this, and I do not know if a Harvard professor would have agreed with me either. I passed the word on because I could remember Oklahoma Indians burning dry buffalo chips for fuel. Clyde and I knew it would work and it did. When soldiers got cold enough, they would try anything to get warm. The infantry wore wet shoes for weeks without removing them. They were warned to remove their shoes to prevent trench feet.

"That experience reminded me of a story when I was a kid in Oklahoma. A politician, was running for an office, and speaking to a group of Indians on a reservation.

"He said, 'If I am elected I will put a house in the place of every tee pee, a spotted pony in every stall, and a buffalo on every hill.'

"The Indians yelled out loud and clear, *'hiya, hiya.'*

"The politician thought the Indians were cheering him on, not knowing what *hiya* meant. Later on, when the old Indian Chief took him on a tour, showing him a pasture where cattle had been, he said to the politician. 'Don't step in the *hiya.'*"

During the months of March, April, and May 1944, Claude and Clyde continued to advance the Oklahoma Wildcat up the boot of Italy, headed for Cassino. The city, with a population of 19,000, was nestled in the valley, surrounded by the mountains of Mt. Castillone, Mt. Corno, and Mt. Cairo. These mountain peaks were great observation posts for the Germans to view all Allied troops as they advanced.

Claude said, "The greatest point of observation for the Germans was atop Monte Cassino. The 1400 year-old Benedictine Abbey was perched on the highest peak and was revered by the Italians and Catholics all over the world. Yet, it was the greatest threat to our advancement because the Germans could see every move we made. [9]

"The Germans had their big guns loaded on a railroad flat-car which could be maneuvered in and out of the side of the mountain. It became impossible for our artillery to destroy the German guns. Thousands of Allied soldiers were losing their lives as the enemy was looking down our throats, observing every move we made. Tanks and other equipment were also being destroyed.

"During these months, about every unit in the American Fifth Army tried to take the city of Cassino and Mount Abbey, including; the 36th, 45th, 34[th]Divisions, and the 1st. Armored Division. Later, the 85th and the 88th gave it a try. Then, came the Fifth New Zealand Brigade, under the command of the British. The British also gave it their best. All these attempts at taking Cassino failed.

"Some units of The 636th Tank Destroyers were assigned to all the above divisions to support their infantry as we tried to advance summit by summit, and yard by yard. Artillery remained the dominant force and each unit was dug in and carefully camouflaged. Green army nets were thrown over the artillery guns while they were not firing, and removed when firing. White nets were also used for camouflage when snow dominated the scene.

Finally General Eisenhower decreed, "If we have to choose between destroying a famous building and sacrificing our own men, then our men's lives count infinitely more, and the buildings must go."[10]

Claude said, "The Allied forces tried everything to keep from destroying the religious Benedictine Abbey, but day after day we continued to mount up casualties."

The bombing of the Abby became a very controversial issue all over the world. It was not the desire of anyone to destroy the institution where monks ministered to refugees who had fled for protection. This was not a very popular move because it was a Holy place where the monks worshipped, and ministered to the people, especially misplaced children. When the decision to bomb the Benedictine Abbey was being put into motion, the Allied Air Force dropped thousands of leaflets warning the town of Cassino and the Abbey of the impending bombing, and when it would take place.

"I agreed with the bombing", Claude said, "When it came to seeing thousands of our soldiers die, because one observation post was being used by the Germans to destroy us, I was ready to do something.

Bombing of Montecassino

"The enemy claimed there were only two German generals inside the monastery, and they did not permit any soldiers within a 300-yard radius; however, the American Air Force spotted two hundred German soldiers fleeing the fortress as over two hundred bombers made their attack on February 15, 1944.

"It is never a pleasure to destroy a religious establishment in the time of war, but we were required to do just that, many times.

Each time we entered a town or city, we shot off the steeples from church buildings. The bell towers were the highest points of observation, and usually contained a German and his machine gun nest.

"Even after the bombings of Cassino and the Abbey, no division was successful in capturing the town of Cassino.

"During the months of March and April, our 636th Tank Destroyers found out how it felt to be bombed by American pilots. We got it two times in one month.

"During the bombing of the Abbey, Clyde and I decided to go to a hill nearby to watch our Air Force bomb. We were about 300 yards from the Oklahoma Wildcat. Just about the time we sat down, I saw four of those B 25s turn left. Clyde yelled, 'They're going to bomb us!' "About that time the bombers went down the draw where we had all our tanks and equipment parked. The equipment got some shrapnel damage, but no one was killed. Clyde yelled, 'Look! Our bedrolls on the tanks have been riddled to shreds.' " Sure enough those American Air Force nuts had made the Oklahoma Wildcat look like a trash wagon.

"A few days later twelve American bombers made another mistake when they flew over, knocking out one of our tanks and wounding several men. It could have been a lot worse, had we not been dug in and protected by some buildings.

"Each of our tanks and heavy equipment were marked with a large American star. We thought the markings were quite visible. The American Air Force made mistakes, which was inevitable in times of war. At the time we were not very forgiving of their mistakes in strafing us with their gunfire.

"After many weeks of constant fighting the 36th Division Infantry was relieved and sent back for rest and replacement of lost men. We, of the 636th Tank Destroyers, continued to support other divisions as they continued the battle.

Allies at Cassino

"We met some interesting people as the Oklahoma Wildcat and crew supported all those different units.

"I recall the French Moroccan *Guoms*. They wore turbans around their heads and blanket-garbed clothing, much like our bathrobes. These huge, black people were from Africa, and fought with machetes and knives. They were very quiet as they slipped around in the trenches, and were very difficult to see because of their total black color. They could scare the daylights out of the Germans, and also us. "It was their policy to slip up on the Germans in a trench, and slit the throat of one, leaving the other one untouched. This put terror in the Germans as they discovered the bodies the next morning.[11]

Clyde said, "Those guys can't slip up on me."

Claude recalled saying the same thing, until he was proven wrong as he related, "One night as I was lying in my fox hole, I felt a hand go around my helmet. I knew it was one of those *Guoms* feeling of my helmet to see if I was German or American. I didn't know how to pray then, but I prayed anyway, that he would not mistake me for a German. The German helmet was square, while our American helmets were rounded. It was their custom to collect ears from one German and leave the other one to view the action that had taken place. The hair actually stood up on the back of my neck! He reassured me that he knew me as he smiled and revealed his snow-white teeth amid his dark skin. I felt the hair on the back of my neck slowly return to its normal position. The Moroccans were not the most dependable soldiers but they could certainly ruin the morale of the enemy.

"We also fought with the Indian Punjab Regiment, under the command of the British Army. They were called Gurkhas, and were a small people who came from the Independent Kingdom of Nepal, India. They fought with knives, and mostly, during the nighttime. We were told that to become a Gurkhas, one had to be able to cut a bull's head off with only one lick.

"I recall them coming by the Oklahoma Wildcat, early in the morning with a pole on their shoulders, carrying four to ten German heads tied to the pole. They received so many days off duty for a certain number of heads. I know it didn't do much for one's appetite at breakfast time, but we didn't have much for breakfast anyway.

"The Scots also fought under the British Command. They were extremely good soldiers as they were fierce fighters and very dependable. They were strange to us farm boys from America, in that they went into battle playing their bagpipes and wearing bright colored kilts, or skirts to us. Clyde and I had never seen men wearing skirts, but we did not dare laugh or say anything about their dress code. I will admit, I felt a little strange in a thirty-two ton M 10 tank destroyer following grown men wearing skirts. We were accustomed to those stripped overalls back on the farm in Oklahoma.

"We also fought with an American-Japanese Battalion, made up of Japanese who were born in America. The majority of them were from Hawaii and California. They had a rough time being accepted by the armed forces because of the bombing of Pearl Harbor. Many Japanese-born people who had become American citizens lived in California, and were put into concentration camps because they were suspected of being involved in spying for Japan.

"This American-Japanese Battalion was first tested in combat shortly after Salerno with the 34th Division. They became known as the 100th Battalion, where they were regarded for their outstanding fighting ability. When the battle got tough, the tough got going. The 100th Battalion was not made up of just average soldiers, they were better than average, ready and willing to offer their assistance to any division in trouble. They were eventually known as 'The Go For Broke Battalion', which was their famous battle cry.[12]

"They proved how truly great they were as they fought side by side with our other American and Allied troops. We learned to appreciate them later on in France, even more, when they rescued the *Lost Battalion*, of the 36th Division.

"The Allied Forces suffered thousands of casualties during the campaign of fighting for Cassino and crossing the Rapedo River. Fighting in a thirty-mile radius for three months, and being under constant shelling had taken its toll on all forces.

"We were glad to get on the move, as the High Command deployed our 36th Division around Cassino, cutting off the Germans at Anzio.

"On May 11, all American Divisions were to take part in a great offensive movement. The 45th Division and 3rd Division had already made the initial attack at Anzio in February, but had been bogged down. In the middle of May, the 36th Division with our 636th Tank Destroyers joined-up with the 45th, 3rd, and 1st Divisions; supported by the 645th and 701st Tank Destroyer Battalions.[13]

"There was heavy fighting on all fronts. The German infantry attacked our tanks with rifles, bayonets, and hand grenades. After capturing some of their prisoners, we found out why they were attacking our tanks in such a fanatic manner.

"'Those Germans are as drunk as skunks,'" someone yelled.

"We found out they were drunk on German Schnapps, something like our wild cat whiskey, the moon shiners made in Whiskey Bottom, near Scipio, where we lived as young boys. Many of the Germans gave up because they were so drunk they were unable to fight. Drinking gave them false courage for only a short time.

"We also felt the wrath of the notorious *Anzio Annie*, the big German 170mm railroad gun with a projectile the size of a bomb. During all the fighting around Anzio, many things happened. Some incidents took place that made us sad and broken-hearted, and some experiences were good to remember as we had a little bit of fun.

"On May 29, 1944, the Oklahoma Wildcat and crew were parked around the corner of a building when we were ordered to pull out and go on a mission. Our tank could not get out because Lt. Driscoll's tank was behind us."

" 'I'll pull back and let you out' " Lt. Driscoll yelled.

"As he pulled his tank back to let us out, he ran over a tank mine, which blew his tank about fifteen feet in the air. Lt. Driscoll, Sgt. Thomas Holcomb, and Private Claude Stratton were seriously wounded. If Clyde could have driven the Oklahoma Wildcat out without Lt. Driscoll moving his tank, we would have been the crew who hit the mine. Things happened we could not explain. Clyde and I escaped injury once again.

Old House at Velletri

"Later, as Clyde drove the Oklahoma Wildcat out of the vicinity of Anzio, with the Germans on the run, we were headed for

Velletri, the last strong-hold on the road to Rome. Our other units were not having any luck pushing the Germans out of that sector.

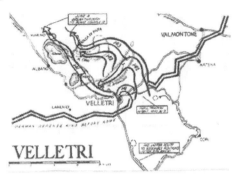

VELLETRI

"General Walker came up with a plan and presented it twice before it was approved. His plan was to take a few infantrymen, assisted by a small tank force, and enter the town of Velletri in the dark of night. His plan was to slip through the German lines, come into Velletri from the rear; and catch the Germans off-guard. No one ever figured how we pulled off that maneuver but we did. The city was captured with our capturing several hundred prisoners and destroying tons of equipment. [14]

"We captured a German band with all their instruments and lined them up in the street, demanding they give us a little concert.

"Someone yelled, 'Play, *Deep In The Heart Of Texas.*' "

"'Nein Texas' ", was the answer.

" 'We said, play *Deep In The Heart Of Texas,*' " many others echoed

" 'Nein Texas, Nein Texas,' " the German prisoners insisted.

Claude chuckled, "Each time they were ordered to play our song, some of the GIs were shooting at the prisoner's feet with machine guns. We didn't ever get our song played, but they did a lot of dancing for us.

"Now another stupid but funny thing happened that made war a little bearable. We had a sergeant who always wanted to fight the biggest, meanest, German soldier we could find. Sgt. Collinsworth was a big, tall, rawboned Texan, and was quite a character. We called him 'Dude'.

" The Dude said, 'Find me the biggest German prisoner and I'll fist fight him fair and square, and may the best man win.' "

"While we were clearing out German stragglers, we went into a cave and captured six German soldiers and one of them was a giant of a man. I knew Collinsworth would be happy that we had found him a match. We were finally going to fulfill his desire.

"I told the Dude we had found a Goliath German and asked him if he wanted to fight him. Dude Collingsworth was ready to fight. Cpl. Sklar spoke enough German, so he explained the rules to old Fritz, the Goliath giant. He understood the rules, pulled off his thick glasses, and the fight was on.

"Cheering was coming from all sides, as our soldiers were pulling for Collinsworth, and the German prisoners were pulling for old Goliath. It seemed to me like they fought for thirty minutes. Both men were as bloody as stuck hogs with bruises and cuts all over their bodies. They became so exhausted; each one finally fell down unable to move and gave up the fight without a winner. I gave old Fritz his glasses and he went off smiling. I always wondered what he told them at headquarters, when they asked him why he was so bloody. Collinsworth never asked for a fistfight again.

"Clyde had the old Oklahoma Wildcat rolling once again, as we headed toward Rome. There were two highways leading to Rome, Highway #6 and #7, which were pretty close together. As I recall we were on one highway and the 45th Division was on the other. The race was on to see which unit could enter Rome first.

"Rome was supposed to be an open city with no fighting going on. It was ready for the taking, and we wanted the Oklahoma Wildcat to be the first one through Rome's arched gate. We learned to be very cautious when going into a new city. Even though we were told Rome was there for the taking, and there would be no fighting; we were not taking any chances.

Rome, Italy

"The highways came together and merged into one before we entered the arched gate. As our Oklahoma Wildcat and crew entered the gate on June 4, 1944, we came face-to-face with the biggest German Panzer tank in the German army. We were not as surprised to see him, as he was to see us. We were no more than fifty feet apart. Before the German tank gunner could set his gun-sight on us we quickly got off the first shot and knocked the tank out. We got another tank with a third one getting away."

"Clyde said, 'Hey! Man I thought there were no Germans still fighting in Rome.' "

"That just goes to show you, not to believe all you hear brother. I replied.

"After the smoke cleared and a very short time of fighting, we were convinced we were the first tank into Rome.

"Later, Capt. Brueckner, our Company C Commander and I decided to scout the area. As we were about to turn the corner of a building to look down the street, a woman hollered out from the window of one of the tall buildings. 'Be careful, there's a machine gun nest up the street.' "

"Her warning was too late. We had just turned the corner when Capt. Bruechner was wounded by the machine gun. Clyde brought the Oklahoma Wildcat down the street, and it didn't take the gunner, Corporal Sklar long to silence that Kraut.

"The woman, who spoke perfect English, had given us the warning. I was intent on finding out more about her as I scouted through the building. She was really happy to see us Americans. She was a New Yorker who had married a native Italian from Rome. They were trapped in Rome during a visit to see his parents. The Italian government wouldn't let them leave, and put her husband in the Italian Army. She didn't know what happened to him.

"After clearing out a few tanks, machine gun nests, and snipers, we drove straight through the city and established defensive positions on roads leading north from Rome. If some other units were ahead of the 141st Regiment supported by our Company C tanks, they did a mighty poor job of rousting the enemy. No brag just facts.

"Oh, well, that was the trouble of being front-line combat troops. We defeated the enemy and kept on advancing town after town.

"The support troops got all the hugs and kisses, flowers, and that kind of stuff. We did all right, I think. We rested a while at a dairy farm and got some fresh milk and butter. To us that was better than all those hugs, kisses, and flowers.

"Well, there was no rest for the weary, as we headed up Highway #1 toward Florence and the Swiss border, getting involved in skirmishes as we went along.

"On June 14, 1944, on the outskirts of the city of Citaveccia, Italy, the odds finally caught up with us. The infantry became pinned down with machine gun fire and asked our tank to help clear out the enemy. Clyde got out of the Oklahoma Wildcat to check out the infantry gun crew we were to assist. When he started getting back into the tank, a German mortar hit the Wildcat, spraying him with shrapnel. This was the first time either of us had been wounded. However, the entire machine gun crew of five men, we had been assisting, were all killed.

"Clyde was bleeding all over his face with the shrapnel still in the wounds. We called for the Medics, pronto, but Clyde knew we could not do a good job without his expert driving. He continued mopping the blood as we knocked out the German machine guns and the infantry moved on out."

Clyde explained, "Sgt. McGuire, the platoon sergeant took me to the aid station where they removed most of the shrapnel. They wanted to send me back to the hospital but I wouldn't go. So many times if you went to the hospital you wouldn't get to rejoin your battalion. I didn't want to take a chance of being separated from Claude and the Oklahoma Wildcat or our crew. Besides, without me around to drive the tank, that crazy Claude would get himself killed with all his schemes he cooked up. Luckily we got released off the front lines that night. We were moved to a location near a field hospital. Where I got my bandages changed each day."

Claude continued. "After Clyde got patched up, he was ready to drive the Oklahoma Wildcat again. Little wounds were not so bad, when we considered the punishment our old tank had received, and she was still going.

"The Germans sat up road blocks along the way toward Florence to slow us down and give them time to establish a defensive line up the road.

"In late June our 636th supported other units and task forces including the 753rd Tank Battalion, 517th Paratrooper Regiment, and the 91st Infantry Division.[15]

"After taking Florence, Italy, the 36th Division was pushing up the coast of Italy nearing the German's Pisa-Rimini defense line when our units were ordered to withdraw and head back toward Rome. I knew something was up but we were following orders. We thought the

Germans may be giving up, or we had gotten to be such good fighters we were going to be picked for some special job.

"As we retraced the miles I could not help remembering how the paths of war changed in our ventures. Beginning at Salerno in September 1943, it had been a snail-like pace through painstaking mountain operations. The miserable weather conditions of rain, sleet, snow, and mud had taken a toll on our troops. There were many rivers to cross and hundreds of towns to take. Many of these rivers and towns were taken over and over again, as we advanced and then retreated.

"It took us from September 1943, to June 4, 1944, to cover the two hundred-fifty mile distance from Salarno to Rome. We captured over 5,000 prisoners, not counting the dead and wounded. The loss in tanks, artillery, and other equipment was a devastating loss to the German Army.

"The month of June was quite a contrast in the type of war and distance we covered. It took us one month to cover the same distance from Rome to Florence, while it took us nine and one-half months to advance from Salerno to Rome. The distance between Rome and Florence, and Salerno to Rome, was approximately the same.

"After ten and one-half months of fighting, we were ready to say good-bye to muddy Italy. There was no doubt in our minds that we had the Germans on a fast retreat. In late June of 1944, we were ordered to a bivouac area near Rome.

"The next five days we rested and performed maintenance on our vehicles. Afterwards, we started loading our tanks and vehicles on ships at the nearby Port of Civitavecchia. We were told that our tank crews would accompany our tanks on the LSTs. Getting separated from tanks had caused a lot of delayed action at Salerno, and we would not forget that lesson.

"We boarded the ship and sailed down the coast line in the Tyrrhenian Sea near Naples. We were never more than two miles from the coastline.

"All of a sudden, we were confronted with a terrible storm. We were under the water more than on top of the water. As we stood on the ship-deck the waves reached such heights we could not see anything but walls of water around us. Our trucks and jeeps started breaking loose from the anchor chains. Nearly everyone on the ship became seasick, even the sailors. The sailors said they had never been in such a tremendous storm.

"I heard about people who got so seasick they turned green. Well, I can verify that is true. I found one of our men sitting in a truck and he was truly green.

"Get out of that truck!" I yelled. "Its' about to break loose and go overboard." "He said in a weak voice, 'Let-err-go.' "

"I managed to get him out and take him below deck to get him some help.   As I returned to the top deck, the truck had gone overboard. Our tanks were located on the lower deck

-"UP FRONT"

By Bill Mauldin

. Our drivers had to sit in their tanks and hold the break down to keep the tanks from causing damage as they banged into the side of the LSTs.

"There were two strange things about that voyage. The storm came up without warning in the length of time it took to snap your fingers. Just as we approached the harbor of Naples the sea became calm as glass. Not even a ripple."

Claude got that far-away spiritual look in his eye as he said. "Now, as I think of that incident, I recall the *Bible story in Matthew 8. Jesus* and his disciples were in a small ship when a storm came up and the disciples thought they were going to perish. They awakened Jesus, whereupon He rebuked the wind and calmed the sea with a wave of His hand. I know now what happened that day, when we were in the storm, as the sea and wind were calmed for our landing at Naples. Miracles of God do happen, even today."

The Stokes twins landed safely at one of the ports of Naples where everyone in the Army seemed to be in a big rush to unload equipment and troops. At that time they didn't know why the rush was on.

The invasion of Southern France and Northern France was planned as a team effort of all forces combined aimed at defeating the Nazi's plan to dominate Europe. The invasion date had been initially planned for May, 1944, but due to the long struggle of eleven months it had taken to defeat the Germans in Italy, the 36th Division plans were altered in their invasion of Southern France.[16]

In the early months of 1944, the Allies bombarded Germany's largest cities with devastating force. British and American fliers had for months been systematically ruining Germany's industrial cities and bombarding military installations on a wide scale in occupied countries. This aerial war, of course, was the prelude to the opening of the real western front. The world has seldom seen such a prolonged period of mounting suspense as that preceding D Day.

Everyone knew it was coming. Roosevelt and Churchill said it was near. The building up of incalculable supply of materials and endless divisions of men in England emphasized it.

There was one false start when the weather, upsetting the best calculations, forced a twenty four-hour postponement after some units actually were on the way to France. They were recalled at the last possible moment. But on the morning of June 6, 1944, General Dwight D. Eisenhower's American troops landed on the Normandy peninsula in Northern France. The landing there preceded the landing in Southern France by two months.

Claude reminisced, "As I look back, the 36th Division proved themselves as mature, competent men in taking the Salerno Beachhead and pursuing the Nazis through Italy. We fought the entrenched Germans through dangerous mountain terrain, out-smarted them in tank maneuvers, and fought under difficult weather conditions. During the hard winter months at San Pietro and Cassino we successfully pulled a sneak attack at Valletri where we captured many prisoners and destroyed tons of valuable German equipment."

The 36th Division was chosen by the High Command to make the initial invasion of Southern France because they were seasoned veterans and proved themselves under extreme battle conditions.

Claude explained, "Our 36th Division was assembled on the plains of the large bivouac area, between Naples and Salerno. We spent most of July in an area southeast of Salerno. The training was extensive as our 636th Tank Destroyers trained with various infantry regiments of the 36th Division in coordinating our methods of support.

"All this training took on new meaning to us. We knew how important it was to learn all we could on all aspects of war. The amphibious landing at Salerno Beachhead had taught us well, the hard way. We were intent upon learning anything and everything that would make us better soldiers. We practiced direct and indirect firing with our three inch fifty guns and small arms.

" Later in the month we had sessions on chemical warfare, map reading, radio operation, and mine detection. We were also drilled on taking part in an amphibious landing. Mistakes in planning had been made at Salerno, but the command had realized the errors. This extensive training gave us renewed courage for future landings. We did not know where we would land, but we were ready."

Before the 36th Division left the plains of Salerno, they marched proudly in review to honor General Fred L. Walker, as his change of command had been moved to Fort Benning, Georgia. This was the first time in over two years the division had taken part in a dress review. They marched with great pride before General Walker, even though they were thinner and war weary, their steps were precise and proud as thousands of soldiers marched proudly in review. Soldiers gave sharp salutes to a general who didn't want to leave, and the men did not want him to go. [17]

Claude said, "We would not forget helping General Walker make his plan of a sneak attack work, fooling the Germans at Velletri. Each G I who took part in that ingenious plan counted it an honor to be included in such a maneuver.

"The 36th Division was to leave the command of the Fifth Army and be assigned to Major General Alexander M. Patch's Seventh Army as we continued our invasion of Europe.

General Walker

"In early August, 1944 we were in the vicinity of Gualiano staging area near Naples, Italy, where our destroyer crews were kept busy maintaining our tanks, trucks, and other equipment. The equipment had to be waterproofed for an eventual amphibious landing. There was no doubt in our minds that we were headed for another invasion.

"For over a month we were thoroughly instructed in every aspect of war. We were well prepared. Most soldiers were weary from battles already fought but were ready to bring the conflict to a victorious conclusion. Were we scared? Yes. A man might appear courageous on the outside but on the inside he has a deep fear of the unknown. Could it be my time to die? A general was asked the question of how many soldiers were scared when they went into combat? He answered, ' Only ninety percent might say they were scared and the other ten percent were lying.' "

"Time could not erase, in our minds, the horrible experience our troops suffered on that first beachhead at Salerno. We could face a new invasion with more confidence because we were now seasoned veterans. Most of us were happy to leave Italy behind. The climate dealt us a blow along with our dealing with the Italian people. We felt as if we could not fully trust them. Actually, we pegged them as being 'wheeler dealers' as they often took advantage of the American G I. Personally, I couldn't forget eating those cats instead of rabbits.

"On August 7, 1944 we moved from Qualiano staging area to our appointed assembly area prior to our embarkation in harbors on the coastline between Salerno and Naples.

"Our Second Platoon of C Company and the First Platoon of B Company were loaded on LSTs. These units were to support the 141st Regimental Combat Team. The First and Second Platoons of Company A were loaded on LSTs on the evening of August 7, and were designated to support the 142nd Regiment of our 36th Division. The 141st and 142nd Regimental Combat Teams were boarded on LCIs on August 8th. All the designated units moved slowly out to sea in front of the convoy. The entire 36th Division was being assembled and loaded as a mighty string of ships progressed across the glassy, calm sea with specific detailed assignments for every man." [18]

It took time and planning to correctly align equipment with approximately 400,000 troops of the American Seventh Army as they waited in line for embarkation. Over 1,000 ships were lined up across the Tyrrhenian Sea from the coastlines of Salerno to Naples.

Claude said, "We shared mixed emotions as we sailed across the open, deep-blue sea. Italy did not look so bad to us as we gazed back at a familiar territory we had conquered. We looked ahead to a land completely unknown to us, as we felt the quivering of butterflies fluttering inside our stomachs; somewhat like our feelings we had experienced in playing basketball or some of those wild horse races we had taken part in during our youth. The flow of adrenaline was at an all-time high."

On August 11, 1944, the 36th Division was afloat. The men learned of their destination on August 13th. Tension began to subside as men kept busy studying maps and charts, along with aerial photos of the designated beaches of Southern France.

Troops headed for France

As the ships moved slowly across the sea some GIs slept, while others performed their duties onboard ship, sunned themselves, checked their gear, and anything to keep busy.

They sailed between Corsica and Sardinia in the Mediterranean Sea, on the last leg of their journey. Tensions mounted again as last-minute briefings were given to every unit, platoon, and squad. Each man was given his individual orders in one of the most precisely planned military operations to be carried out.

The Seventh Army, led by Major General Alexander M. Patch, was confident of the Divisions selected for the southern France Invasion. The VI Corps' Assault Team...the veteran 3rd, 36th, and 45th Infantry Divisions including all the support units.

Meanwhile, the Germans were in big trouble in northern France, when in late July in Normandy, the breakout at St. Lo was developing. There was no doubt the pressure was on in full force.

In southern France, the German forces had been greatly reduced to meet the serious threat of coastal areas in northern France. The Germans, with thirteen divisions, was forced to reduce the number of divisions to nine. However, the reduction gave them a more streamlined battle force if they could concentrate all the divisions in one area. This was impossible with the Allied forces hitting them from different directions.

The Germans knew of an impending invasion of France from the south, but they were uncertain of which beach landing the American forces would choose and when the invasion would take place.

On August 13, 1944, Major General John Ernest Dahlquuist received a flashed message, in his room aboard the command ship:

"D-day, 15 August 1944; H-hour, 0800 hours."

Claude said, "The 36th Division was directed to four beach areas: Green, Red, Blue, and Yellow. The 141st Infantry Regiment was spearheaded for Green Beach supported by B Company and C Company of the 636th Tank Destroyer Battalion.

"We looked toward the Southern France coastline with great anticipation and confidence, being assured this would not be a repeat of the beachhead at Salerno. Our crews on each tank were well prepared to meet the challenge."

-5-

World War II – Invasion of Southern France

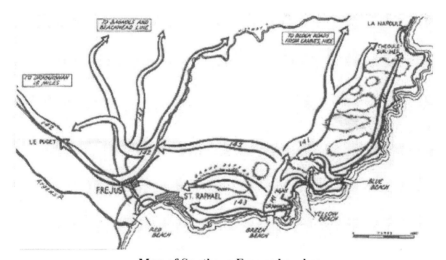

Map of Southern France beaches

Seventh Army Patch

On August 15, 1944, The American Seventh Army, led by Major General Alexander M. Patch, made the Decision Day Invasion of Southern France.

At 0800, The 36th Division, 141st Infantry Regiment spearheaded the first landing in Southern France on Green Beach, supported by the 636th Tank Destroyers.

Prior to their landing, reconnaissance identified the potential obstacles American Forces might encounter. Much of the shoreline was filled with the German's under-water hazards, such as casements of ingenious defense mesh, calculated to intercept and entangle men and equipment. Mines were also a potential threat.[1]

Claude's memoirs continue. "The rumble of guns from Allied ships echoed up and down the white sandy beaches of the French Riviera. Airplanes were zooming over-head with bombs dropping on the white-bleached beaches up and down the front. Well-designed colorful hotels and French café's were dotted along this chateau-studded Riviera vacation spot of Europe.

"What an invitation to thousands of war weary American GIs who deserved a good change of pace. Mademoiselles and good food would have to wait. The division was not quite ready for a vacation, but we did hope to return for some rest and recuperation after we chased the Germans out and returned this beautiful country to our French allies.

"Our troops were confident that this invasion would not be a repeat of Salerno. We felt planning had been done from the first to the last detail. We clearly understood why our tanks were loaded on designated LSTs in line with the 14lst Infantry. The Southern France invasion was a great improvement over Salerno. Our tanks were right there, ready to support the infantry.

"Our infantry regiment was already assembled on LCIs and headed for Green Beach. The infantry is at its most vulnerable point before the smoke barrage has cleared from previous naval bombardments on shore. This smoke barrage often hinders visibility, preventing them from seeing underwater entanglements. The men met with little resistance due to the German's concentration of troops on the other three beaches.

. 36th **Division lands**

"The Germans were also surprised by the American Forces landing on Green Beach because to them it was a potential trap. The beach was 250 yards long and fifty yards deep, flanked by a cliff with a wall of stone to the left, rock formations and granite jutting out on the right, and backed by a sharp incline near Cape Draggmont. Our High Command outsmarted the Germans again with this surprise choice for a spearhead landing.

"The assault on Green Beach, by the 141st Infantry at 0800, led by Col. John W. Harmony striking to the right, with his 2nd Battalion, and the 3rd Battalion to the left met with slight resistance due to the surprise landing.

"After only forty minutes of fighting, our C Company's, 2nd Platoon, and B Company's, 1st Platoon were ready to support the infantry from their rear.

"Clyde pulled the Oklahoma Wildcat out in front as we unloaded from our LST. The infantry had already cleared the beach and taken up positions to advance.

"Our Oklahoma Wildcat was the first tank destroyer on the beach of Southern France. This landing was quite a contrast to our previous landing at Salerno's dirty, muddy beach where our tanks forded water to go ashore. On the French Riviera our tanks were unloaded in nothing flat on a dry, white, and sandy beach in the area of the beautiful city of San Raphael. Our tank crews were ready for action. We knew what kind of fighting we might encounter and we were ready.

"Our M10 tanks tackled those steep inclines that appeared impossible to climb. We were confronted with German machine gun nests, which had outposts of observation in tact and mortar guns ready for firing.

"That little problem didn't worry us much for this invasion seemed like a breeze compared to Salerno. Things were really clicking together with the combined efforts of all support units.

ONE ROCKEY STRIP

"Engineers quickly pulled bulldozers and other heavy equipment in line to remove heavy boulders, rock formation, and other obstacles as they made wide openings for our advancing equipment and troops."

Yellow Beach was a small horseshoe inlet near the small town of Agay and next in line to be taken.   The plans to take this beach were abandoned because it was so small and carefully defended by the German's submarine mine netting and was not worth the time and effort. Loss of lives and equipment was the greatest consideration.

Meanwhile, the 1st Battalion of the 141st Regiment met heavier resistance on Blue Beach where German anti-tank guns opened attacks on landing crafts carrying American troops and equipment. However, this resistance was quickly overcome as the small battalion of destroyers pushed the Germans from their rocky, dominating cliffs, capturing 1,200 prisoners and forcing them to surrender. The battalion was awarded a *Presidential Unit Citation* for this action.[2]

At 0945 hours the 143rd Infantry, commanded by Col. Paul Adams landed on Green Beach with the 1st, 2nd, and 3rd Battalions turning west behind Red Beach, defeating the Germans to gain the high ground northwest of Drammont, paralleling the shoreline toward San Raphael.

Red Beach was located near the resort town of San Raphael, where an airport was located near-by. This sector was most important to the entire Seventh Army because this area was the central source of supply for the Germans. Yet, it was also the most heavily fortified with all the underwater obstacles, land mines, heavy gun placements and fortified concrete pillars, which concealed machine gun nests.

Naval guns fired on Red Beach starting in the early morning, on August 15. Demolition crews attempted to rid the beach of land mines, but were foiled in those attempts. The Germans continued to delay landing on the beach with all their fortification working for them.

At 1100 hours the 142nd Infantry Regiment started their first wave of men toward Red Beach as the Navy heavily bombarded the coast again. Special demolition boats proceeded ahead of the troops as they tried to clear a pathway through all the entanglements. Many of these boats were fired upon and sank.   The infantry was headed for disaster.

Radio communications were broken between the 36th Division Commander and the Navy Commander, Rear Admiral Spencer Lewis, who was in command of the Task Force carrying the 36[th]Division. Commander Lewis made a courageous, timely decision to pilot the 142nd Infantry landing onto Green Beach, which had already been cleared. This action probably saved hundreds of men from death.[3]

Claude continued. "Actually, Green Beach became the real gate-way for the thousands of 36th Division troops landing in Southern France. The141[st] Infantry made the initial spearhead landing at 0800 on August 15, 1944, and had Green Beach secured by 1000 hours.

"The 142nd Infantry entered through Green Beach at 1530 hours and proceeded to go northwest behind Red Beach paralleling the drive of the 143rd to the south, as they headed for the capture of the all important towns of San Raphael and Fregus. Fierce fighting continued through the night. By early morning Red Beach was secured.

"There was quite a contrast between the Salerno, Italy Invasion and the Southern France Invasion. In a matter of hours all four beaches were secured. After over a week of fierce fighting at Salerno, our troops were still trying to defeat the Germans for control of Italy's beachhead, with the loss of thousands of American troops, while casualties in the Southern France Invasion were cut to a minimum.

"Many things contributed to our successful venture; great planning by the High Command, the assembling of troops and equipment together, and the element of our surprise landing. Fighting with experienced veterans through Italy made a huge difference, as well. With nine months of combat in Italy, the 36th Division supported by the 636th Tank Destroyers were tried and tested and proven to be one of the best fighting units in World War II."

"Marseille, France, one of the largest seaports in the world and France's second largest city, flanked the eastern tip of a 100-mile stretch of beach along southern France. The Allies made their second invasion of continental Europe with great success

"There is never an easy invasion, as men are killed, wounded and maimed for life. Hearts harden as men witness destruction of church buildings, homes and businesses of innocent people, plus seeing hungry and displaced families in a state of despair.

"The 143rd Infantry entered the city of San Raphael where hundreds of Germans surrendered. Our tank destroyers blasted obstacles protecting Nazi pill- boxes manned by fifty-two Germans.

Sgt. Durwin P. Mayo directed our Oklahoma Wildcat through the ruins as we continued supporting the infantry.

Sgt. Durwin P. Mayo

"On August 17 and 18, 1944, Clyde and I with the Oklahoma Wildcat, were assigned to a task force made up of infantry tanks, tank destroyers, a reconnaissance company, engineers, and a medical company. Our Company C of the 636th Tank Destroyers was assigned to Butler Task Force in this particular campaign.[4]

"The race through Southern France was on. It was good to be on level ground away from mountains and rivers. Our tanks could do the job we were trained to do. We advanced some days, thirty, forty, fifty, and as much as one hundred miles in one day. One might think we were fighting Germany's rejects. Not so, we were fighting the German 19th Army with the support of their 11th Panzer Division, Hitler's best.

"Ironically another tough enemy was the American Air Force. We were bombed and strafed almost every day by friendly fire. I still give the old American Air Force boys in my Bible class a hard time about this error. The fault was not all theirs. If we hit a pocket of resistance the officer in charge called the Air Force and gave them the location to bomb and strafe. Sometimes we cleared out the resistance before they got there, putting us ahead and past their target. The pilots thought we were Germans retreating. The only thing was, those pilots must have been color-blind. We had orange sheets on the back of our tanks and we threw out smoke grenades that were suppose to tell them we were Americans. Well, this was war.

"The infantry didn't want us tank guys around either. That is, until they got penned down with machine gun fire or wanted a pillbox destroyed. They were plenty glad for us to clean out snipers from a window in a tall building but they just didn't like all the artillery fire our presence was drawing toward them. Shucks! I guess we could understand their little problem.

"I recall an infantry captain asked me to fire a round of high explosives at a big white rock. He told me the Germans had his platoon pinned down near the rock.   I fired at the rock and in a little while the medics brought the captain's 1st sergeant down on a stretcher.   Now, I felt real bad about that, until the sergeant said, 'Thanks for this million dollar wound. You just got me out of this mess and back to Fort Worth, Texas.' "

Claude concluded, " I hate war and my wife Madlyn hates war." Echoing similar words of Franklin D. Roosevelt and Eleanor.

"As Clyde and I continued across beautiful France, many roads and highways were lined with trees on each side of the road-way. Some trees were cut down as the Germans used them for roadblocks, trying to slow our advance, and giving them time to push ahead in their fast retreat.   Engineers did a fantastic job as they cleared the roadway in a very short time.

"It was a shame to disturb those beautifully landscaped highways with their trees so perfectly spaced and all the same size. Our engineers cut the trees and used them in building roadways. They could have both sides of a road cleared in a hurry and with such perfection as the trees fell in order, crisscrossing trees in the roadway.

" *The Caissons Went Rolling Along* as we took town after town, staying close on the heels of the Germans. As front-line troops we were in hot pursuit having little time to enjoy the liberation of the French people.   They were most sincere in their appreciation for having been liberated, more so, than were the Italians. All along the way they tossed flowers and fruit at our passing tanks and jeeps. Many of them spoke good English as they expressed their gratitude over and over.   Here again, we missed a lot of those hugs and kisses that some rear echelon dude got because we had to keep moving along.

"The Free Fighting French were great allies as they continued to assist our troops throughout our advance keeping us informed on the location of German troops. They had maps in hand, which designated German traps ahead.   Our necks were saved many times as they appeared on roadways to give us information. A number of women were in this group of fighters who showed no mercy on the Germans who had conquered and defiled their country.

"On one occasion, we were stopped by the French fighters by the side of a road. A good looking French woman, who was dressed in shorts, held a sub-machine gun in her hands as she prodded another French woman in front of her. We stopped to ask what was going on.

They had captured the woman helping the Germans as they tortured and killed eight American prisoners.

"Someone said, 'Turn her over to us we will use her to our advantage.' "

"With a sudden whirl and a 'rat-a-tat-tat', the beautiful machine gun Annie took care of the situation as she mowed her down right in front of us. Who knows? Some of the men may have used her to cook, clean, or something.

"As we liberated town after town, it didn't take long for the French to flush out the German sympathizers. They shaved the women's heads and marched them down the street, ridiculing them by kicking, spitting, and calling them names. We continued to see this several times a day as we captured towns and cities along the route the Germans had taken as they retreated toward the German border.

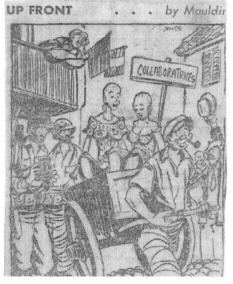

(Picture to Right)
."I'm gonna' send this home and scare my gal outta' foolin'around wit' garrison sojers'…"

"On August 22, 1944, we took the beautiful university city, of Grenoble, nestled beneath the French Alps. At first the French could hardly believe the long-awaited Americans had finally arrived. They loved the sight of the big burly Texans, perched on top of the M 10 Tanks and our infantry as they marched down their fine avenues with officers sitting proudly on jeeps and other equipment. The liberated yelled, 'Welcome to you all! 'You from Texas, Oklahoma, New York, San Francisco, Ohio, Illinois, or Alabama… 'Thank you for ridding us of the Germans and the nightmare of four years under their rule.' " [5]

"By the seventh day we had advanced 250 miles from San Raphael to Grenoble. The 36th Division and our 636th Tank Destroyers had to leave Grenoble as rapidly as we had entered. We received reports of a buildup of German forces near Montelimar. Our division was assigned to deal with an immediate threat as we headed north, where the Germans were trying to take a big stand in the vicinity of Montelimar. This sector covered the Rhone Valley to the Swiss and Italian borders.

"The 36th Division advanced through town after town crossing road-blocks, capturing many prisoners and destroying the enemy as we advanced on our mission. On one occasion, we captured a German officer riding a motorcycle with a sidecar attached. Sgt. Glen McGuire decided to take a little ride into a near-by town to scout the Germans.

"'Stokes, let's take a little ride and have some fun,'" Sgt. McGuire, coaxed.

"I decided to rest instead. When he returned the Germans had shot the sidecar off where I would have been riding. Saved again!

There arose a few problems as we progressed at such a fast pace. Equipment, supplies and new replacements were not keeping up with our troops. As we stopped at night, we usually replenished the required necessities.

"Most of the time, our rations and second lieutenant replacements came at the top of the list. By this time, second lieutenants were replaced frequently, as they did not last long and none of the men wanted to be one, because the Germans picked them out as their main targets. Many of our best sergeants were offered a battlefield commission, but most of us turned it down. We knew the score. Being a second lieutenant was a big joke to us.

THE ROAD BACK

By Bill Mauldin, American legion News Service

"We recalled how second lieutenants, and even sergeants came to us with fancy neon stripes on their uniforms and helmets designating them as officers. We told them if they wanted to stay alive they better get rid of those stripes and marks because the Germans would have them cleared out in no time. As we proceeded many discarded stripes lay on the roadway.

"On August 22 and 23, 1944, there was heavy fighting in and around Montelimar, as the 36th Division was closing in on the desperate Germans who were trying to prevent a breakthrough in their lines.

"Our Company C was supporting the attack on Montelimar, as well as maintaining road blocks outside of St. Marcel and in the vicinity of Puy St. Martin. During the day we destroyed eighteen vehicles belonging to the famous 11th Panzer Division.

"On August 24, in the early night, the enemy launched a counter attack on our Company C. We lost two tank destroyers and had thirteen men wounded in the attack: Lt. George M. Hess Jr., Sgt. Howard J. Dikeman, Sgt. Durwin Mayo, T4 Charles E. Shipley, Capt. Stanley V. Lucas, T5 William R. Jacoby, T5 Lester E. Wold, Pvt. Vitctor Walanski, and Cpl. Daniel S. Sklar. In the midst of this battle we destroyed one Mark IV Panzer.

"We got word that the Germans were trying to break through our lines and make an escape route. All units were alerted and many destroyers were shifted around to meet support needs. Our 636th Destroyers were divided up at this time. Captain Downs of our C Company led two of our tank destroyers to a strategic area of battle near St. Martins. We joined our tanks with Company A as we continued to set up roadblocks to prevent Germans from escaping."

On the morning of August 25, 1944, amid a fierce battle near Grane, an artillery shell knocking off a track and at the same time hit the Oklahoma Wildcat, wounding Lt. Charles F. Hall, and Sgt. Claude H. Stokes.

Members of the 36th Security were also wounded; Privates Jack R. Morris, Henry P. Champney, Raoul J. Dufresne, Willis R. Legget, Charles W. Wien, Arthur L. McCauley, Victor Walaneski, Milton Cagan, and Nicholas Cordisco. [6]

Claude confided, "I think it hurt me more to see my tank destroyer being dragged off than me being hauled off. It had not been a good week for the Wildcat or me. Cpl. Sklar was wounded earlier in the week. Without my tank and gunner I felt a great loss.

"The Field Hospital medics said they took out fifty-three pieces of shrapnel from my back and legs. Both legs had pretty deep gashes in them. The medics just sprinkled a little sulfa-powder in those holes and applied bandages. I stayed around the field hospital for three days. An old tank man had work to do.

Claude in the hospital

By Bill Mauldin, Stars and Strips

"Meanwhile, Clyde was still in one piece and was busy getting us a replacement tank. There was one thing you could say about the motor pool; they could always repair your tank or find a replacement.

"In times of fighting, we also had time for a little fun. Boys will be boys. Our tank had the responsibility of guarding a bridge over a river as we chased the retreating Germans. We looked down the road leading to the bridge and noticed a sharp left turn to get on the bridge. We could see vehicles coming at least one-half mile before they got to the bridge. Instead of shooting at the vehicles, we decided to shoot behind them as they approached the bridge. When the Germans came to the sharp turn they speeded up causing them to approach the bridge in full throttle. Instead of going on the bridge, they ran off the road into the river.

"We thoroughly enjoyed the scene as motorcycles with the sidecars attached, carrying a driver and an officer, plunged into the river. The driver bent over trying to outrun our bullets. We could see their facial expressions quite well as they came to the curve, realizing they could not make it on the bridge. We shouted in glee, 'Into the river they go!' In a few hours we almost had that river dammed up with Germans and their vehicles.

"It wasn't all fun and play. From August 15 to August 30, 1944, the Germans paid a terrible price with 11,000 casualties, 2,100 vehicles destroyed, 1,500 horses used to pull artillery guns were killed, and six 380mm railroad guns were destroyed. Even with these losses, the Germans still fought well. I don't know about our infantry losses, but the 636th Tank Destroyer Battalion had seven men killed and seventy-six wounded. We lost thirteen destroyers, two jeeps, and one personnel carrier.

"During some of the fiercest fighting, the Germans damaged the Oklahoma Wildcat, resulting in our having to send her in for repairs.

"Meanwhile, we began fighting with a replacement tank destroyer as we continued to support the infantry. For three days, on the outskirts of a town, the Germans were trying to re-take the town when they knocked out our tank.

"The Germans continued their counter-attack pushing us back. We began fighting on foot with the infantry. The Germans were only a few hundred yards behind us. A new replacement gun loader from my crew was fighting beside me. After all these years I cannot remember his name, but I do recall that he was a tall, blonde fellow from Georgia. We came upon a mortar crew. It was apparent that a shell had landed in their nest, killing all of the crew, but the mortar was still in place.

"I asked my companion if he had ever fired one of the mortar guns.

"With his southern drawl, he quickly answered, 'N-o-o s-u-h.' "

"Me neither, but we're going to learn how together.

"I knew you adjusted the tripod to lower or raise the barrel, pulled the firing pin on the shell, dropped it into the mortar barrel, and fired. I adjusted the barrel almost straight up since the Germans were very close. I told my buddy to pull the pin and drop the shell in place. He did but the shell didn't come out as fast as he thought it should. He started to lean over the barrel to see why the shell had not fired. I grabbed him and yanked him back in the nick of time.

We got pretty good and managed to fire all the shells that were left in the nest. We slowed the Germans down, killing and wounding a good number of their troops. Not bad for two old tank men who didn't know how to fire a mortar. On the battlefield, you will try anything to stay alive."

Claude and Clyde recalled another battle that was very alarming to their family back home, but could not remember the date it happened or in what area of France it occurred. They did recall the Oklahoma Wildcat had been heavily damaged prior to this incident and had been sent in for repairs. During all their combat they had four replacement tanks knocked out by direct fire, destroying the tanks. The Oklahoma Wildcat went in many times from blown tracks and other repairable damages.

Claude told the story in his own unique style. "As we fought trying to retake a town our tank was knocked out after it received a direct hit. Luckily, no one was hurt seriously while we were escaping. The new replacement on our tank, having been with us only a couple of days, was plenty nervous when we lost the tank. We continued to fight with the infantry and were in no big hurry to get back to our company. However, the replacement went back to the Company Headquarters in a hurry. When they asked him where the rest of the crew was, he told them we had been killed or captured.

"Company C checked and found the tank without any dead or wounded and assumed the remainder of our crew had been captured. They reported us as missing in action. When we showed up the next day, they had to go through all the paper work again, saying we had been found.

"That incident taught us a lesson about not reporting in as soon as we could. Our anxious folks, with three sons in constant combat had been keeping the postman busy, getting telegrams to them every few days.

"We finally put the Germans on the run again as we advanced eighty miles from Montelemar to the beautiful city of Lyons, France. On September 2, 1944, we were assigned to a combat patrol sent into Lyons to see if the Germans had destroyed all the bridges across the Rhone River, which ran through the city. As our troops entered the city we knew the enemy was gone because the French people came out by the hundreds. They swarmed our tanks and vehicles expressing their thanks.[7]

"It was a good thing the enemy was gone because there was no way we could have fired our guns with all those people on our tank. Besides that, I didn't have a crew. The French Patriots were entertaining them with food and parties of celebration. In a few hours they returned fed, happy, and ready to continue the fight.

By late September of 1944, the Germans became more organized and started to defend each city with more shelling. Cities became larger and harder to take. Some of those cities and rivers were Uesoul, Luxeuil, the Doubs River, and Moselle River. It seemed like Company C was always on the roads where the Germans set up roadblocks. We destroyed one only to find others ahead as we advanced.

"Our Oklahoma Wildcat proceeded toward a wooded area near the Moselle River when we noticed a German soldier running into the woods. He was a good distance from our tank when I fired a round of 3/50 explosive at him. All of a sudden I heard someone hollering. Our commanding officer, Col. Wilber and Maj. Gen. John E. Dahlquist walked beside my tank and the general said, 'Sergeant! You surely didn't shoot that big gun at one German soldier?' "

"No Sir; General, I was shooting at that 40mm gun in the woods. Now to be honest, I didn't dream there was a 40mm gun in those woods and I didn't think the two officers would follow us into the woods but they did. I think they wanted to see if I was lying to them. When we captured the woods a 40mm gun had been destroyed. I didn't do it but I was proud someone else did.

"General Dahlquist turned to Colonel Wilber and said, 'That sergeant has the best eyes in this army.' Years later at a reunion in Nebraska, Col. Wilber asked me, 'Did you shoot at that German or did you actually see that 40mm gun?' I had to confess the real truth. With a twinkle in his eye he said, 'Through all these years I knew it, but I had to ask.' " (In 2001, we were watching a World War II movie, when General Dahlquist referred to the sergeant who had such good eye-sight.)

Claude commented, "The 36th Division continued to push forward in October, although our number of troops was depleted. We were content to fight with older equipment, but the newer divisions coming into battle had improved equipment. Morale of our men was very low.

"Rest for our war-weary bodies was far in the past. We kept looking for a break so that we could pull out of constant fighting for just a breath of rest. However, our infantry waded through seasonal rains and eventually snow that chilled them to the bone. The Germans never ceased firing from their dug trenches. We seemingly had nothing to look forward to but mountain after mountain, defended by minefields, artillery, and mortar fire.

"While we were trying to secure our position in the Vosges Mountains one of our M10 tanks became disabled, whereupon the Company Commander told Clyde, Sgt. Sklar, and me to go down after dark and evaluate the situation. We were to drive the tank out, or destroy it. I decided to keep that valuable tank out of German hands. As we came upon the M10, I went aboard while Clyde and Sklar stood watch. It was evident that some crew had to make a quick departure, as empty shell cases and other debris were scattered around. We were trained to know where every switch was in the dark. As I turned the switches, that old tank purred like a kitten but I was unable to get it in gear. After removing the debris from around the gear mechanism, I found a can of pork and beans from a *Five-In One-C Ration* lodged at the base of the gearshift, preventing it from being put in gear.

"Clyde and Sklar were not too happy about my driving that M10 out of the valley in the dead of night, but off we went. When we entered the road around the hill from whence we had come, they sure did voice their opinion. That road was barely wide enough to support the tank with deep ravines on each side. Clyde shouted, 'Claude you are going to get us all killed and send this tank to the bottom of one of these ravines.' I told him to get on one fender and Sklar on the other. They were instructed to tell me when the tank began to slide off the roadway. Both men did plenty of yelling from both sides. I was determined to drive that thirty-two ton baby back to headquarters. Wow! We made it.

"Clyde doesn't like to remember this incident because he thought no one else could drive a tank like he could and I really couldn't drive as well. He was the best.

"Progress through towns like Bruyeres, Biffontaine, and Belmont became very slow. Most of the time we fought from house to house, and block by block until towns were taken. The key fighting was not along the roads and in towns and cities, but around the hills and through the beautiful Vosges Mountains where the Germans possessed the greater advantage.

"Our tank destroyers continued to support our ground troops through the mountains where thickets of tall pines and underbrush gave the Germans cover as they seemed to have a mine under every leaf and a gun nest in every thicket of the forest.

CLEARING THE VOSGES HILLS

"In a week's fighting our troops captured six hundred forty-five Germans and that many were also wounded.

The Corps Commander decided it was time for the 36th Division to make an all out push to reach the Meuthe River from St. Die to the north. We were given the mission of seizing the long spur running in a southeasterly direction east of Biffontaine and north of the Neune River, to protect the right flank of the corps effort. Execution of this mission resulted in one of the most dramatic episodes of the war, *The Lost Battalion* of the 141st Infantry.

"On October 23, 1944 the infantry sent its 1st Battalion forward to take the high ridge and ground over-looking La Houssire. On a thickly wooded hill, two hundred seventy-five soldiers were spread out in a three hundred by three hundred fifty yard area, digging their foxholes deep, using knives to whittle down trees to use as cover, and folding blankets around the trees so they wouldn't make noise. They were quiet because they knew they were cut off with approximately seven hundred Germans around them.

"The battalion was cut off for seven days with very little food, water, ammunition, or medical supplies. Their pleas for help came from their only existing radio. Efforts to save them from the Germans came by soldiers trying to break through the German lines. The air force tried dropping supplies but failed to get them to our troops. We even tried shooting supplies in by artillery. All efforts failed.

"Finally, on October 30, 1944 the Japanese-American 442nd Infantry Regiment, was designated to break through the German lines and attempt a rescue. They had proven themselves as great fighters and were incorporated into a regiment with two other Japanese-American

Japanese-American 442nd Infantry

battalions. Their slogan: '*Go For Broke*', clearly identified them to all our troops. Our 636th Tank Destroyers, Company C, 2nd and 3rd platoons were chosen to support the 442nd in the daring rescue. And we did. We were eager to fight with the 442nd again. In Italy they were known as the 100th Battalion.

They were the best, but the only problem of fighting with them was; they were so small and very good at camouflaging themselves, making it hard to see them in the Vosges underbrush. The Germans had the same problem.

"As we proceeded through the thickets, we captured a German soldier. We normally turned prisoners over to the infantry, but you couldn't see one of those little camouflaged infantrymen; therefore, we had to put the prisoner in the tank with us. As we continued to fire our gun, shell cases fell to the floor of the Oklahoma Wildcat. Our German prisoner picked them up and threw them out of the tank for us. The 3/50 shell cases were so hot he was burning his hands, so I showed him how to pick them up by the base end, thus, preventing him from getting burned. He liked that bit of instruction and was making a real good member of our crew.

"We all got busy and sort of forgot about old Fritzy, until I felt him tapping me on the shoulder and pointing in front of our tank. None of the crew had noticed a German trying to set up a bazooka right in front of the Oklahoma Wildcat. He was having problems making it fire. Now a bazooka was a nightmare to tank men. He was so close our gun could not get that low.

"Thanks to Fritzy, the problem was solved as he handed me a grenade. I pulled the pin and threw it out and that took care of the bazooka man. Old Fritz was elated and so was I. He saved the lives of all the tank crew plus his own.

"The infantry finally took him off our hands as he went away, smiling and waving good- bye. Actually, I hated to see him go because he was handy to have around. I think with a little training, he might have made a good tank commander.

"The Germans finally pinpointed the whereabouts of the Lost Battalion when the belly tanks of medical supplies and rations and batteries began hitting the target at the same time. The two hundred seventy-five lost men were told to conserve their ammunition until they were sure of their target. The Germans rushed the sector where the battalion had concentrated most of its heavy machine guns. The enemy took an awful defeat as they lost hundreds of men from artillery and air bursts in the trees.

"It wasn't long until the 442nd Infantry made their first contact with the Lost Battalion. Were they ever glad to see those little guys coming up the hill. Sgt. Edward Guy, of New York City, was on outpost as he looked down the hill to see the first infantryman coming up for the rescue. The sergeant leaped down that hill like crazy, yelling and laughing with gratitude as he grabbed the little guy in a big bear hug. Pfc. Mutt Sakumoto just looked at him with a lump in his throat and said, 'Do you guys need any cigarettes?' The remaining two hundred seventy-five men were overjoyed to see those little guys come for the rescue. Job well done by the *Go For Broke Boys,* and Company C of the 636th Tank Destroyer Battalion.[8]

"The Vosges Mountains were tough on everyone. The engineers had a difficult time with snow, rain, mud, and trees across roads. Land mines and booby traps were everywhere.

"One night we pulled off the main road onto a side road to spend the night. The heavy snowstorm had completely covered the ground. The following morning, when we were ready to move out, I walked out in front of the tank to inspect the surroundings. I noticed a dark spot in the snow about six inches in front of the track of the Oklahoma Wildcat. As I removed some snow I found two tank mines stacked together. If we had moved one foot, I would not be telling this story today. That type of explosives would have blown that tank and crew to Kingdom Come. Wow! Saved again.

"The Vosges Mountains were beautiful and unusual with thickets of tall pine trees covered in blankets of snow. The snow actually floated down in huge snowflakes as big as your hand covering the ground in a short time. Many times the GIs dug their trenches and put a shelter half-tarp over the top. In no time the snow would completely cover the trench enclosing a very warm sleeping quarter. In the stillness of the night you could hear a sound for miles.

Beautiful Vosges Mountains

"One night a brazen German soldier, challenged any American soldier to come out and fight him as he stood atop a Vosges hill. You could hear his voice loud and clear for miles. I don't know if he had read the story in the Bible concerning David, in First Samuel: 17. A Philistine giant of a man challenged the Israelite Army to send out a soldier to fight him in a similar situation.

"We later received an army newspaper called *The Stars and Stripes*. The news reporter related, 'David slew the Philistine giant with a sling shot and one smooth stone and an American soldier got his giant with one bullet and an M 1 rifle.' "

"In November of 1944, it was a cold, wet, snowy and a bloody month for the 636th Tank Destroyer Battalion. Through this phase of fighting, we lost more men and tank destroyers in this month, than any other, since our landing in France.

* * *

"During the first week in November, President Franklin Delano Roosevelt won his fourth term in office as the President of our United States. Harry S. Truman was elected as Vice- President. Clyde and I had been in combat for over a year, but we were too young to vote."

* * *

"On November 28, several tanks were parked around a building where a number of our infantry was located. Hostile troops infiltrated around both sides of the house, and at daybreak they opened fire with machine guns, 20mm guns, and bazookas. The replacement tank occupied by Claude, Clyde, Corporal Sklar and one other crewmember, received a direct hit from bazooka fire, which immediately burst into flames.

Forced to leave the vehicle, the men sought refuge in the house. Upon reaching the cellar they discovered six wounded infantrymen who were left behind when the friendly troops abandoned the building. The house had already been set afire by the hostile shelling.

Being aware that the wounded faced certain capture or death by burning if left in the building, Sgts. Claude and Clyde Stokes, along with Sgt. Glen McGuire, valiantly assisted in an immediate evacuation of the men. They braved direct small arms and shellfire to carry them across one hundred twenty-five yards of exposed terrain to a place of safety. By making two trips to the house, they saved all the injured soldiers in spite of the great personal risks involved. For this heroic achievement in combat, they were awarded the *Bronze Star Medal.*[9]

Claude often commented on the bravery of Sergeant Glen McGuire who was the commanding sergeant over his 2nd Platoon. Many times he asked for volunteers to make daring rescues of soldiers in trouble. Clyde and Claude were always ready to assist him as they had great respect for his decisions. Sgt. McGuire was not a demanding commander but showed deep concern for the welfare of all the men with whom he was associated.

Claude said, "I lost more than a tank, even though it was not the Oklahoma Wildcat. I lost two extra forty-five caliber pistols I had picked up on the way. I sort of borrowed some ivory from a store and worked for a month making ivory handles for those pistols and I almost had the job completed. I hated to see my fancy pistols burn up in that replacement tank. Oh well, I didn't need to look like General George Patton anyway."

After ninety-two consecutive days of combat in France, the 36th Division Infantry continued to battle their way through the most narrow and steep passes in the Vosges Mountains, which the Germans considered almost impregnable. The 36th Division was determined to finish the Germans off, continually setting their eyes on Alsace as they led the Americans toward the German Fatherland.

Claude disclosed, "In four months we had moved the Germans from the white beaches of the French Riviera, to the thresh-hold of their own country. I might say, the 36th Division and the 636th Tank Destroyer Battalion earned a spot in history as the first combat units to cross the Vosges Mountains from east to west against a determined enemy.

"The Germans were great fighters and we knew they would defend Germany even more so than their conquered territories, but we were ready to finish them off and return to our own United States of America."

-6-

World War II – Invasion of Germany

    In December of 1944, Major General, Alexander M. Patch continued his command in Leading the Seventh Army against the enemy.

    The 36th Division with its three regiments covered a wide front all up and down the length of the area going from France into Germany.

    Claude continued his memoirs. "Fierce fighting continued on all fronts as we gained entrance into Germany. The Meurthe River was swollen from recent rains, which made the crossing most difficult.

Our units' encountered heavy resistance from troops concealed in elaborate trench systems; the approaches were mined and heavily snarled with barbed wire obstacles.

"During the month of December we took many German cities and towns. Towns were captured, only to have the Germans make a counter attack and retake the town. This happened over and over, slowing down the advancement. The cities of Selestat, Betche, Mittelwihr, Colmar, Strasbourg, Bischwiller, Rohrwiller, and Oberhoffen were only a few of the cities we conquered. It took us several days to take the largest city of Selestat. Between our taking Selestat and Betche, the Oklahoma Wildcat was sent in for repairs that resulted in our fighting with a replacement tank.[1]

"On December 13, Company C supported the infantry and took the town of Mittelwihr. The Germans made a counter attack about dark, breaking through our infantry lines. Tank destroyers were cut off for a while during this heavy fighting. Our tank received a direct hit by a large artillery shell. If an artillery shell hit on one side of the tank and then on the other side, we knew from experience, the third artillery shell would zero in on us. I opened my mouth to avoid a concussion from the explosion. I received shrapnel wounds in my mouth, face, and neck. The rest of the crew escaped without injury but the tank caught on fire and burned.

"We took shelter in a cellar underneath the house. There were five or six men from our platoon, five or six from the 753rd Tank Battalion, and eight or ten infantrymen trapped in the cellar. A jeep was parked by the cellar door, which was set on fire by the Germans. Our only exit was lit up as big as Dallas, Texas. We were in quite a predicament.

"Everyone began discussing whether to stay in the cellar and surrender or try to fight our way out. When I landed in North Africa I promised myself I would never be taken prisoner. Clyde and I both said we were going to shoot our way out. Our gunner, Cpl. Sklar, and several other men in our Company C decided to go along. Sgt. Glen McGuire, our platoon sergeant, echoed, 'I'm with you guys. Let's go!' "

"The chances for our men escaping through that lighted tank and jeep in the doorway and Germans surrounding us was slim to none. Sgt. McGuire was the first one out and was killed instantly.

We lost the best platoon sergeant in the Army. Company C had six men wounded and two killed.

"Our men darted here and there, dodging bullets and Germans as we tried to make our escape into the wooded area, firing as we proceeded. Things were in a state of chaos as we fought our way into the darkness and joined others who escaped from that area. A second lieutenant dressed in a nice combat suit was among the group of men. Everyone was in a pretty big hurry as we attempted to crawl through a barbed wire fence with only one opening. Now the lieutenant was being careful not to mess up his nice combat suit. As he started crawling through the fence he got hung in the only opening. He was right in front of me and was holding up the line of men behind me. I finally put my foot on his hindquarters and gave him a little help to get him through which resulted in tearing his nice combat suit.

"When we got back to the Command Post, he told our Company Commander I kicked him through the fence and wanted me court-martialed. There I stood with a bloody face and my mouth had begun to swell. I wasn't a pretty sight at all. The captain, sizing up the situation, turned to me and asked me to give my side of the story. After I finished, the captain jumped up, pulled his pistol and said to the lieutenant, ' you - - -, I ought to shoot you myself. You could have cost me a good sergeant and a good tank crew!' That made me feel better but I don't think it did much for the lieutenant."

"I still have some rearranged teeth, one dead tooth, and a piece of shrapnel in my neck to remind me of December 13, 1944, and Mittelwihr, Germany.

"On December 14, we borrowed a tank from one of the other platoons. Lt. Jones, Cpl. Sklar, Clyde, and I assisted the infantry to retake the town. When we got to the place where we lost our tank and jeep, we found the bodies of all the men we left in the cellar, plus our good friend, Sgt. Glen McGuire. The Germans lined up the men from the cellar beside the burned jeep and tank and killed them. I might say, there weren't any prisoners taken that day."

Numerous times, over the years, Claude told the story of Sgt. McGuire getting killed. At one time he admitted crying when they lost him. Evidently next to Clyde, he was his best buddy. He often expressed the desire to share his great admiration of Sgt. McGuire with some member of his family but never has been able to contact any of them.

Claude continued. "It seemed we were constantly retaking ground we had previously taken from the Germans. The Germans threw everything at our troops on all fronts as they fired heavy artillery and mortar concentrations against us. Their artillery literally demolished the streets in every town. For three days the Germans unceasingly harassed our infantry with mortars. Mine fields blocked us many times as demolition crews were called in to destroy the mines. Veterans of the 36th Division continued to move the enemy out of their positions, despite our war-weary bodies.

"The Germans brought many of their troops across the Rhine River trying to stop our advance. They had a terrific casualty toll inflicted upon them in men killed, wounded and captured. Finally, after the Germans had bombarded us with everything they had, we turned the tide and put them on the run.

"Our 636th Tank Destroyer Battalion was scattered over a wide area as we supported different infantry regiments and often times other divisions. The infantry regiments were fighting in many different towns at the same time. Our tank destroyers assisted the infantry, not as a complete company or platoon, but in some cases as one tank. Our tanks stood by radios ready for a call of support to any unit.

"Our Oklahoma Wildcat and crew were assigned the job of guarding the crossroads leading into Riquewihr. We decided to set up housekeeping in a house nearby. The previous occupants were not present when we moved in so we just made ourselves at home. When it got dark, a mother with two young daughters came home. Needless-to-say, Mom wasn't happy that we were there. But then, we weren't over there to make the Germans happy. We tried to be nice to them as we gave them some of our C rations. The girls enjoyed the chocolate candy bars. They seemed to like our company but Mom didn't like that either. Every morning they left and came home at night. While they were gone I searched the house for weapons because I just didn't trust Mom, however I never found anything.

"Two days later the Germans counter attacked and our infantry was pulled back from the area. We too, were ordered to retreat down the road away from the house in which we had been taking refuge. As we were leaving I kept seeing and hearing bullets ricocheting off the

Oklahoma Wildcat. I told Cpl. Sklar there was a German sniper somewhere close by and to keep out an eye for him. In a little while he said, 'that's no him! 'That old lady in the house is shooting from the upstairs window.' I don't know where she had that rifle hid, but I do know she failed on the rifle range or I would not be telling this story. Too bad, I rather liked the old mom. If she hadn't fired that rifle, she might still be around today.

"On December 19 and 20 we moved to Strasbourg. This German town sat on the banks of the Rhine River separating France from Germany. In peacetime, France occupied Strasbourg on one side of the Rhine, while Germany occupied it on the other side.

"Strasbourg was blessed with the world's finest cathedrals. Most of the towns in Germany had town squares where the people took care of business.

The mayor of the city called the people together and made his announcements or speeches from this designated place. [2]

Strasbourg

"It so happened there was a music store on Main Street. The music store had a huge balcony overlooking the town-square. About ten of us Company C boys borrowed some of the music store's instruments and made up a band. We chose all kinds of brass horns. We didn't know a tuba from a trumpet. Neither did we know a note of music. We paraded out on that balcony and began our concert blowing with all our might. We blew till we gave out and then one of us made a big speech. About all we could say was '*Viva la France*' and '*Nein the Bauch.*' Of course we spoke a lot of English in the speeches telling them what we thought about old Hitler.   Then we blew on those horns again. It wasn't long till the town-square was full. We drew a larger crowd than the mayor. We did a lot of bowing and blowing while we had a lot of fun. Let's face it. Some musicians have the ability to draw a crowd and some don't.

"Strasbourg was peaceful compared to the rest of Germany bordering France. The people roamed the streets. In comparison, the women out-shined the short dumpy women in Selestat. There were plenty of young, pretty girls who were well dressed. Actually the German people, as a whole, were more like Americans. I personally liked them better than the Italian and French people.

"On December 24, 1944, the 36th Division and the 636th Tank Destroyer Battalion got a great Christmas present. We were being relieved from the front lines. Wow, after one hundred and thirty-three days of combat without relief, we started celebrating. Our division had been fighting on the front lines since August 15, 1944. No other unit in any war had ever fought that long without rest and a bath. We really looked forward to a good rest, a bath, shave, haircut, and some clean clothes. This was a most welcomed gift.

"We drove the Oklahoma Wildcat and crew back to a designated rest area located near Harbouey. Now, we had formed a little plan. We had to make a stop to pick up another present we had previously found in a haystack. We uncovered a bright, shiny, black car, which one of our tank crew was glad to drive back to the rest area. We had great plans for that car.

"On the way to the rest area we came upon a Red Cross doughnut vehicle. The Red Cross women pulled over and stopped for us to get by them. We took that as a real invitation. After one hundred and thirty-three days on the front lines, our mouths were watering for a good old doughnut. We piled out and asked them for some of their doughnuts. The lady in charge said, 'Oh, we can't give you any of these doughnuts. We don't serve combat troops. We are taking them back to the hard-working men at the Rear-Echelon.' " "That did it! I drew out my old trusty Thompson machine gun, patted it a couple of times, let the safety off, and she handed over the doughnuts in a hurry. We drove on with our shiny new car and the Oklahoma Wildcat just as happy as we could be. Later, those Red Cross ladies reported us. The officer in charge told us the women would drop the charge if we gave them the shiny black car. Oh well, you win some and lose some. There were no more, *Bonnie and Clyde*, episodes for us. Even today, I don't have much respect for the Red Cross.

"Our 636th Tank Destroyer Battalion finally arrived at our designated rest area in the afternoon of December 24, 1944. Man, we were ready for that first night's sleep. After one hundred and thirty-three days of combat, it took quite a while to get us guys de-loused and cleaned up. We had forgotten how it felt to be clean again with fresh clothes and dry feet.

We felt pretty secure in the rest area without all the battling going on around us. The First, Third, and Seventh Armies were located across a three hundred mile front. Many divisions were engaged in battle a good distance from us, giving us a sense of security. We were wrong again.

"We just got settled in, when we were awakened from a deep sleep. The Germans had dropped their paratroopers right on top of us. Now I couldn't believe they chose us instead of all those other divisions. We spent all night chasing those Krauts in hand to hand combat. Usually, something happened in every disappointment that turned out for our good.

"The paratroopers were members of a German bicycle brigade. We captured the paratroopers plus their bicycles. The bicycles were a good cash or trading item. We took advantage of both.

"After five days our long deserved rest came to a sudden end. Like I always said, there is no rest for the weary. On January 2, 1945, we were put on alert and stand-by orders. The Germans were attacking on all the Seventh Army fronts, including the Belgium Bulge and Bastone,

"On January 3, our 636th Tank Destroyers were back in heavy combat. It was extremely cold and snowing every day. We painted our tanks white so as to blend in with the snow. Then as we advanced from one town to another the snow seemed to disappear. Our white tanks showed up for miles. We covered the white tanks with mud until we got back in the snow again. Washing that mud off with snow was no fun.

Snow covered tanks

"We continued to encounter fighting in the cities of Bitche, Hauenau, Enchenberg, Lemberg, Goetzenbruck, Montbrann, Herrlisheim, and Weyersheim, to name a few. We not only supported our 36th Division Infantry, but the 100th and 79th Divisions, plus the 12th Armored Division."

In times of war, young soldiers are called on to do dangerous and sometimes almost impossible tasks as they face combat. Sometimes it requires bravery, special skills they were taught in training, special pieces of equipment, and sometimes it requires all three; bravery, skills, and equipment.

Claude and Clyde have forgotten many battle stories in the above towns, but one incident stands out above all others in Claude's memory. This story is about one tank commander, Sgt. Claude H. Stokes; one tank driver, Sgt. Clyde T. Stokes; one gunner, Corporal Daniel S. Sklar; and one M 10 Tank Destroyer; The Oklahoma Wildcat. Last but not least, the story concerned about one hundred 36th Division infantrymen, and one German underground machine gun pillbox.

Claude tells the story in his own way. "This story is still fresh in my memory, even though it happened fifty-six years ago. On January 12, 1945 in the town of Enchenberg, Germany, our Company C, 636th Tank Destroyer Battalion was supporting the 143rd Infantry of the 36th Division. On the outside edge of the little town of Enchenberg, was an open field about three-fourths of a mile wide, with a line of trees behind the open field.

"As the infantry started to cross the open field the Germans let them get to within two or three hundred yards of the tree line when they opened fire with heavy artillery and a mortar barrage. They were also firing machine guns and rifles from an under-ground bunker. This bunker not only served as a machine gun nest but a perfect observation post. All this resulted in penning our infantry down, causing a heavy casualty count.

"The commanding officer called down a heavy barrage from our own artillery and mortar fire without any results because the bunker was under-ground with a thick concrete and steel top, covered with soil.

"The officers decided that the only solution was to get close enough to the bunker to fire into the slits or openings of the bunker where the machine guns were located. How to do this little job was the big question. If they tried sending the infantry to throw hand grenades or fire rifles into the bunker, it would be suicide; many wounded and dead soldiers already lay across the field, which proved to be an unwise choice.

"An officer commented. 'How about sending a M-4 tank out there to do the job?' But they didn't have a one available. Another said, 'A tank destroyer could do the job.'" " The officers finally agreed that the only chance of saving the one hundred infantrymen was to send a M-10 tank destroyer in to do the job. The officers sidestepped giving a commanding order to a tank destroyer commander but decided to ask for a volunteer.

"Word came down for all tank commanders to meet. Now we didn't know what was going on or what kind of problem the Division commander had. They said, ' "We need a volunteer to go knock out a pill box with a machine gun nest that has our infantry pinned down in an open field.'" "We learned to be cautious before volunteering for anything in the Army, but I thought, *not a big deal. They have our infantry pinned down and I have knocked out machine gun nests before. Besides, I have the best gunner and tank driver in the company.* So-o-o, I volunteered our tank crew to do the job, not realizing the impact of the situation. However, I knew the tank crew would be ready.

"I strutted back to the Oklahoma Wildcat, with great confidence and told the crew I had volunteered us to do a little job of knocking out a pillbox so that we could rescue around one- hundred of our infantrymen. They all echoed, 'No problem, let's go.' "

"As we moved out of town to the edge of the open field, I saw at least six high-ranking officers from the infantry, plus Capt. Latham, our Company C commander. I thought to myself. I have made a mistake volunteering for this detail.

"When I saw and heard what we had to do, I knew I had made a big-g-g mistake.

"As Captain Latham, with tear-filled eyes, came over and shook our hands and said, 'You guys are great soldiers,' I knew I had made a huge mistake."

"The plan was simple, they explained. 'All you have to do is go across the open field and get close enough to the bunker to put some 3/50 rounds of high explosive and a few armored piercing into the side of the bunker, knock out the machine guns, and do away with the observation post.' "

"I could see our crew was facing a mighty big problem. First, half of the German Army awaited us just beyond that open field. Second, a tank destroyer had an open turret, making it easy picking for German mortar fire. The life of a tank commander and gunner would last about two minutes in a situation like that. Third, I asked the officer about all the wounded and dead who were lying across the open field. We certainly didn't want to run over them in a thirty-two ton M 10 tank. He assured me his infantry would take care of that.

"There was another thing bothering me. They all talked in terms of getting out there and knocking out the pillbox, but no one said anything about getting back. I'm convinced that there was not an officer in the crowd who thought we could go out there and do the job and get back. Their only hope was to get the job done. The loss of one tank and crew was a small price to pay to save the lives of one hundred infantrymen. And I knew that was true. That is, as long as you were not a part of the tank crew.

"Well here was the final plan. We decided to use only a three-man crew to do the job. Once we were there I would be the loader for the gunner, Cpl. Sklar. We laid fifteen rounds of 3/50 high explosives and fifteen rounds of armored-piercing on the floor of the tank for easy access. Clyde's job was to get all the speed the old Wildcat had, and I might add she was the fastest tank in our C Company. My job was to make sure every round of ammunition hit the mark.

"Each of us knew what to do. We set off to do the job. Clyde backed the old Oklahoma Wildcat back into town about two hundred yards so we could get up full speed before the Germans knew we were coming. We hit the open field and when the Germans realized what was happening, they opened machine guns and artillery bursts of fire with which they were experts.

"An Artillery shot over an open-turret tank was bad news. Once there the teamwork started. In a matter of seconds we had pumped thirty rounds of 3/50 shells into that bunker. I believe every round went into the bunker. Now it was up to Clyde and the Oklahoma Wildcat to get us back to safety. And they did. Only the Good Lord knows how we lived through that battle. I'll admit the old tank received some more battle scars, but she was okay.

"One officer said, 'I didn't know those tank guns were automatic.' "

"Our guns are not automatic," I bragged. "Just a great gunner.

"He declared, 'It sounded to me like they were automatic, after firing thirty rounds in twenty-seven seconds.' "

"Now I don't know about the twenty-seven seconds. In most cases that kind of mission would have earned a medal, but what we received was more rewarding than any medal we might have gotten. We had the good feeling of knowing we had defeated the enemy that day as we saved the lives of many of our fellow comrades and we had done what we had been trained to do. An added reward came days later when we again supported our infantry in battle when one of the infantrymen passed by us and read the Oklahoma Wildcat sign. He said. 'You guys saved our butts last week...Thanks.' "   "That was more rewarding than any medals we could have been given."

The above incident was reported by First Sgt. John Fruwirth of Company C, and also mentioned slightly, in the great book by Tom Sherman, *Seek, Strike, Destroy;   The History of the 636th Tank Destroyer Battalion.* [3]

The 636th Tank Destroyers continued to encounter fighting in the cities of Bitche, Hauenau, Echenberg, Lemberg, Goetzenbruck, Montbrann, Herrlisheim, and Weyersheim, to name a few. They not only supported the 36th Division Infantry, but the 100th and 79th Divisions, plus the 12th Armored Division.

Claude continued, "Many times we yearned for a break to stretch outside the tank. One evening we pulled over where some of the infantrymen were dug in during a lull in the fighting. We decided to try stopping for the night. Pfc. Lawrence 'Shick' Silbernagel was a member of our tank crew at the time. Now Shick had a problem with sleepwalking. We started to get a few winks, when old Shick decided he had better have a little talk with the infantryman who was on guard duty.

"As he peered down into the fox hole he saw a hollow-eyed, weary soldier who had about a month's heavy growth of beard and long hair. Shick drawled, ' Soldier, I thought I should tell you that I walk in my sleep.' "

"The infantryman looked up at Shick, spat his tobacco juice over the trench, patted his faithful rifle, and warned, 'Buddy, you better not walk tonight.' "   "Pfc. Silbernagel came back to the tank and tied strings to his fingers and anything he could think of to anchor himself down to the tank. He made it through the night but he did have quite a time untying himself when we got ready to leave.

"We were proceeding through another German town when an enemy sniper kept firing on us. After we eliminated the sniper and investigated the area in which he was located, we saw a pen sticking out of the sniper's pocket. It was a fancy pen with the name 'Lawrence Silbernagel' engraved on it. I commented to Shick that he might have killed one of his relatives. I should not have said that because the incident really did worry him. His folks were from Germany... Who knows?"

An interesting story has been told in many 36th Division books, including, 'Seek, Strike, Destroy', by Tom Sherman. I also had the story in Claude's scrapbook, which I saved from a California newspaper, taken from The Stars and Stripes of the 36th Division's T-Patch news.

The articles describe the incident as having taken place when the Germans were attempting to retake the cities of Strasbourg and Saverne. It had been a seesaw endeavor on the part of the Allies and Germans as they tried to hold on to conquered territories, involving an arc of cities and towns from Rohrwiller to Weyersheim. Units were shifted to meet the threat of Germany's Tenth Panzer Division.

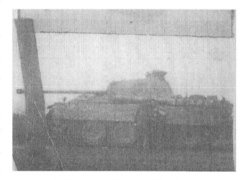

A German Panzer Tank

The 143rd and 142nd Rigiments were slammed right into the middle of the attack committed to drive out the Panzers. The area was partly wooded and gave over to open space, ideal for armored fighting.

Claude related, "Our 2nd Platoon of the 636th Tank Destroyers were labeled as 'The Armored Devils' by the printed stories." One such story follows: [4]

Outnumbered, "Armored Devils" Blast Seven Enemy Tanks

They deserve their title of, "Armored Devils", the sharp shooti'n veteran gunners of the 636th Tank Destroyer Battalion. They proved their right to it when the Germans tried to break out of their bridgehead north of Strasbourg. Out-numbered 5 to 1, these men drove off the enemy, cost them seven tanks, and never gave them a chance to get off a single retaliatory round.

The Battalion Commander, Lt. Col. Charles Wilber, Hollywood, California, explained the battle: "We had to be geared for extremely fast action," he said. "It was a case of the guy who gets in the first round being the victor. We got in the first round. Jerry never got a chance to fire back."

The warning net alerted Company C three hours before the German tanks ground into range. The Third Platoon, commanded by 2nd Lt. Lee Kiscadden, Lebanon, Pennsylvania, was employed along a heavy thicket with a clear field of fire in three directions. Two guns were there, about 20 yards behind the infantry. The enemy tanks slid out of a tree line about 2,000 yards to the east. The T-Patch TD men moved toward the edge of the woods and waited

The driver, Cpl. Lem J. Luke, Tifton, Georgia, marked the enemy's progress. "Yonder they go," he repeated. The enemy tanks kept coming. They crossed a small bridge and stopped.

Col. Wilber was standing next to Lt. Kiscadden. "When are you going to shoot?" He asked impatiently. Lt. Kiscadden was standing next to the destroyer driven by Sgt. Rufus Brantley, Temmile, Georgia. He called Gunner Cpl. Wiley Johnston, Alpine, Alabama, "When you're ready."

The enemy tanks were sitting ducks; halted just across the small bridge about 1200 yards away. It was Sgt. Brantley's first combat as a tank commander. The day before he had been a medico and a private first class. He spotted what he later described as the "biggest ---- on earth." Two rounds smashed into the tank, two columns of orange fire and black smoke roared into the gray snowy sky. His monster was two Mark 4s sitting hull to hull. They were both destroyed.

Sgt. William Rutledge, Houston Texas, spotted two other tanks at the same time. Short a loader, he had to observe fire and handle the gun by himself. Two Tiger tanks had forced their way past the infantry defense line and were 2,000 yards across the plain, going towards the rear. Rutledge poured three rounds into one, shifted his fire and hit the second. The second tank withdrew the first one was crippled. Another round disabled it.The Third Platoon had accounted for three tanks in less than two minutes. The left flank of the open field was secure.

Lt. John Kehoe, of New York City had his Second Platoon on the edge of a town where his three guns covered the open space from the right flank. He was in an observation post directly behind his destroyers when he saw two groups of enemy medium and heavy tanks come into sight in front of the tree line, at this point about 4,000 yards away. The first group was the larger, seven tanks. All told there were twelve.

It was a large order for the three guns of the platoon, but the men were waiting for a chance to even an old score. In the last action, their platoon sergeant had been shot out with his fourth tank destroyer.

Sgt. Claude Stokes, McAlester, Oklahoma, watched from the turret of his "Oklahoma Wildcat," driven by his twin brother Sgt. Clyde Stokes. The enemy was still 3,000 yards away when he opened fire. "We had to peel them off," he said later. "They were shooting up our infantry." He spotted a Panzer tank when the artillery dropped a smoke shell behind it. Silhouetted, it made an ideal target.

Claude in the Oklahoma Wildcat

US Army Photo

But the first kill went to S/Sgt. Leonard Collingworth, Dodd City Texas, who had been sitting watch in the Oklahoma, Wildcat. The Panzer tank was a sitting duck, 2,500 yards away.

It looked like easy shooting. It was phenomenal. Across the snow and against the gray sky, the tanks were barely visible. The range, while not excessive, was very long. As the colonel said: "But those boys, they handle that three-inch gun like it's an overgrown rifle. They are deadly accurate."

When Sgt. Stokes took over the "Wildcat", Sgt. Collingsworth led two mounts down to an alternate position where they had a better field of fire. Frustrated, German tanks and infantry had shifted their attack and were trying to slip into the town from the flank. Sgt. Hester Bently, Cullman, Alabama, and his gunner, Cpl. Harry L. Beatty, Saxton, Pennsylvania, caught two tanks out of eight that had stopped to fire at the infantry. They drove the first back to the tree line, knocked out another with three rounds. The others left the position, taking their supporting foot troops with them. Sgt. Harvey Hale, Fairmont, West Virginia, spotted another tank that tried to lead a large number of infantry flanking the town. As it stopped to fire on our troops dug in along the road, Sgt. Hale pumped five fast rounds into it at the almost impossible range of 3,000 yards. When the tank caught fire, he traversed to pile up the enemy infantry around the tank. On the right flank, the three guns had accounted for four tanks and countless enemy infantry, plus one tank damaged. On the left flank, the two guns had knocked out three tanks, and crippled another. S/Sgt. Warren G. Stedman, Warren, Arkansas, had gone to lead up supporting tanks, but by the time they got there, the area had been secured. The Germans never attacked again.

* * * *

Claude said, "The Stars and Stripes gave our 636th Tank Destroyers a little credit. Back home in the States, about all you could hear about was what was happening up north in the Battle of the Bulge. We were fighting our guts out with those Germans in the south, but very little was said. Many of the GIs complained up-a-storm.

"We were still supporting our infantry, but progress was slow. So many towns and cities to take like; Rohrwiller, Gambsheim, Bischwiller, Niederschaeffolsheim, Herrrlisheim, Oberhoffen, and

Hagenau. None was easy taking as the Germans were making their last stand. They were fighting on home soil. It made a big difference to them to see their own homes and towns destroyed.

"The month of February brought some changes for the 636th Tank Destroyers. We began receiving the new M 36 tank destroyers with 90mm guns. A and B Company got them first but only a few at a time. I didn't think I could give up the Oklahoma Wildcat.

"Things started to slow down some during March as the Germans had suffered a great loss in men and equipment. But they could and would put up a good fight. They proved that in the town of Oberhoffen. After two or three days of fighting we captured the town. On March 11, we were parked beside one of the few buildings left standing. It had a basement that made a good safe haven from mortar and artillery fire. Our crew decided to settle in for a while in the basement and take a breather.

"At about 7:30 p.m. we got a phone call to report to Company Headquarters by 7:00 a.m. the next day.

Oberhoffen, Germany

Clyde and I were going home. Wow, that was great news for us. We would not have to give up our Oklahoma Wildcat tank for one of those M 36 jobs. We knew the battalion had a plan in motion sending one or two men home per month on a forty-five day furlough. The plan was to send the old men first, not by age, but by how long they had been in combat. There were only eight or ten original men left in our unit, out of approximately one hundred twenty-eight men, who had landed at Salerno. Clyde and I were two among that unit to make it through to that point of the war.

"On March 11, 1945, after 365 days of combat, in the town of Oberhoffen, Germany, Capt. Latham told us we had been chosen to go home. We were going home through the new point system. Wow!

"This was the last town and the last days in combat for Clyde and me as members of the crew of the Oklahoma Wildcat. We were excited at the good news of going home. We could hardly wait to tell our other tank crews in Company C, who were also resting in basements about a block or two down the street. We got about halfway to our destination, when the Germans opened fire with artillery and mortars.

"Clyde panted, 'I don't know about you, but I'm heading back to that basement where it's safe and I'm not getting out until tomorrow when I'm going home.' I echoed, I'm with you Brother."

"When we got back to the basement and the firing stopped, I tried the phone and it wasn't working. I knew the shelling had cut the line so I decided to go outside and try to find the break and repair it. While I was trying to find the break, the shelling came toward me from all sides. A piece of shrapnel ripped across my chest, tearing a big hole in my jacket, went through my shirt pocket, and took a big chunk out of a Scrip/to pencil in my pocket. That pencil probably saved my life. I still have the pencil to remind me of how close I came to not going home the next day.

Claude's Pen

"As I said, the house in which we were staying was the only one standing in that area. Well, the next morning it wasn't standing either. I think those Krauts got wind that we were going home. You would think they would have been glad.

Pfc. James Stubblefield, and
Cpl. Daniel Sklar, personal photo

"The next day we said good-bye to our buddies, Cpl. Daniel Sklar, Pfc. James Stubblefield, and the great, old battered Oklahoma Wildcat. I told the guys to take care of her and she would take care of them. The faithful old tank had been shot up so bad on two occasions, she had to go in for major repairs. While we waited for those repairs, four other M 10 replacements were knocked out. "I knew we were leaving the Oklahoma Wildcat in good hands, but it was sorta' sad to leave her behind. This was our last time to see the old gal.

"We checked out a lead on her in the year of 2000, from our good buddy, Thomas Holcomb, Mount Pleasant, Texas. We discovered he was having a bout with cancer and was only dreaming about the tank, I suppose many other World War II

'The Oklahoma Wildcat TD

Veterans may dream or remember in some way, the 'Oklahoma Wildcat'.

"We left Oberhoffen and headed toward Laharve, France. Upon our arrival we stayed in an under-ground mountain cave the Germans previously occupied before the Normandy Invasion. The next morning, when I awakened, I discovered I had lost my voice in the damp cave.

"After losing my voice, Clyde had to do all the talking. Each time we were addressed, we were to give our name, rank, and serial number. Clyde, for once, got to do all the talking as he repeated the required answers to questions. Clyde, as spokesman worked. We were put on a small ship and routed to England. As Clyde and I sailed for England and looked back toward Germany, we were confident that we would not have to return again. It was evident that the Allied Forces had defeated the Axis.

"Upon arriving in England, we were informed that our being awarded the Silver Star Medal, entitled us to fly home, but we would have to wait until there was a flight going to the United States. They said it could take as much as a month, but we could take a ship and leave sooner. Clyde asked, 'Which one is leaving first?' They pointed us to the *Queen Elizabeth*, anchored in the harbor. We headed for the ship; ready to get started with no fooling around with the air force.

"As we waited on the dock to be checked by an army captain, I saw men trying to take home everything from machine guns to 81mm mortars. The only thing I wanted to take home was a pair of German binoculars, which was better than American. When the captain spied them I saw his eyes light up and I thought, here *goes my binocular*. He said, 'I have to take those binoculars, but we will mark them and you can have them later.' I hope he didn't think I was that dumb, but I was not going to argue on that day.

"To make matters worse, the Red Cross girls had given me a cup of coffee. Standing on the dock one was subjected to the sea gulls as they flew overhead. I believe this one sea gull had not had a 'b. m.' in days because he dive-bombed my coffee cup and filled it to the brim. I wasn't going to ask the Red Cross for another cup. It had been only a couple of months earlier when *The Red Cross* and I had a difference of opinion as we took doughnuts from them at gun-point when they refused to give us dirty, nasty, smelly, bunch of hungry, combat soldiers a measly doughnut. Who knows? One of them may have been on that dock. Besides that, I couldn't argue with them because I still couldn't say a word. After we cleared the Army inspection station, we headed for the Queen Elizabeth and boarded her, ready to get back to the greatest land on earth, the good old 'United States of America'."

The Stokes Twins had fulfilled their destiny in World War II. They had fought a good fight. They had finished their course. The forty-five day furlough would be continuous as the war in Europe ended with the destruction of the Axis powers in less than two months.

On May 7, 1945, at 2:42 a.m., Germany surrendered unconditionally, to the Western Allies and Russia. The surrender took place at a little red schoolhouse at Reims, France, which served as the headquarters of General Dwight D. Eisenhower. Chief of staff, Lt. General Walter Bedell Smith signed in the absence of General Eisenhower. Representatives of U.S.S.R., France and Great Britian were present for the surrender. General Gustav Jodl and General Admiral Hans Friedeburg, represented Germany.

The surrender brought the war in Europe to a formal end after five years, eight months and six days of bloodshed and destruction, and was signed by, Colonel General Gustav Jodl, the new chief-of-staff of the German army. [5]

The Germans were asked sternly if they understood the surrender terms imposed upon Germany. The answer was, "yes."

Germany, who began the war with a ruthless attack on Poland, followed by successive aggressions and brutality in interment camps, surrendered with an appeal to the victor for mercy toward the German people, and armed forces.

Nazi Germany began as an outgrowth of economic and political maladjustment following World II; and it wound up as the symbol of most of the modern world's crushing ills. There were many evil men in Nazi Germany, but to the outside world, four stood head and shoulders above their fellows as the epitome of all the Nazi party represented. Those four were Hitler, Goering, Goebels and Himmler. Germany's dream of world conquest came to a shattering end with the collapse of the Reich, which Adolph Hitler boasted would endure a thousand years.

The civilized world was sickened by the atrocities in Poland in 1939, as Hitler with three evil officers, attempted to annihilate the Jewish people and other peoples not fitting into his madman scheme of producing a super-human race.

On May 7, 1945, The Oklahoma City Times Newspaper gave a tremendous summary story entitled, 'Exit the Frantic 4', from the

Associated Press. The newspaper pictured the four evil men who led in the greatest atrocities against innocent people of all time.

Heinrich Himmler was known for his cruelty in the commitment of millions to concentration camps all over Europe, both in Germany and Axis held territories. American soldiers were appalled as they viewed the skeleton bodies, dead and alive, as they marched along side the internment camps.

EXIT THE FRANTIC FOUR-EXTRA
Hitler, Goering, Goeble, and Himmler leaders came to a shattering end with the defeat of Germany's Reich. Associated Press- Oklahoma City Times Newspaper, May 7, 1945

Claude said, "I have talked with fellow-servicemen who related to me that after fifty-six years, such horrible scenes of atrocities could not be erased from their memory."

The collapse of Germany brought an end to the European phase of the Second World War to be fought in this century. A war with an estimated cost of one trillion dollars in money and more than six million men lost.

Claude concluded. "In World War II, the 36th Infantry Division, alone, had the third highest casualty list of any American division, which numbered, 27,343, of whom 3,974 were killed, 19,052 wounded, and 4,317 missing in action. [6]

Remember?

EXTRA
Associated Press-
Oklahoma City Times
May 7, 1945

ATROCITY

The war began when Germany invaded Poland in September; 1939. This date also marked the start of Nazi atrocities that sickened the civilized world. Here is a typical scene. Polish peasants have been forced to dig and then stand in their own graves while their executioners prepare to shoot. The European war is over, and even the terrific job yet to be done on the other side of the world cannot obscure the fact that the allied nations are over the hump in their fight for survival against axis barbarity. In the cataclysmic events of recent weeks it is easy to forget some of the milestones on the long road that led to victory. A few of those milestones are pictured on this page. The polish invasion seems far back in history now. So do Dunkerque,

Dieppe, the bitter plains campaigns in Russia and the historic siege of Stalingrad. The London blitz, and later the reverse blitz against Cologne and Berlin areacvient stories. So are Tunisia, El Alameine, Cassino, Salerno and Anzio. But all were Major phases of the struggle. The events they symbolize stand already as the things, which shaped this world's destiny for many generations to come.

REMEMBER THEM!

-7-

World War II – Back To the United States of America

On March 15, 1945, Claude and Clyde embarked from a port in England, aboard the *Queen Elizabeth*.

Claude related. "All returning servicemen were divided into groups. We were assigned to Camp Chaffee, Arkansas, along with six other men from Oklahoma and Arkansas. All men were assigned to army camps located in or near the state in which they lived. Each group was given different tasks to perform while en-route to America. We were the smallest group and were given the job of repairing any bed or bunk that was broken or damaged on the ship. We repaired about five beds on the whole voyage, so we got off easy where detail was concerned. However, we did encounter hundreds of men who were wounded and appeared to be unable to help themselves.

"There was a big advantage to being in a small group and having the run of the whole ship. Each man was given a card with a number on it. The mess hall, one to five, was registered on the card. We were given a class A card, allowing us to eat at any or all the mess halls. I might say, we ate at all of them. We couldn't seem to get filled up. Besides, we remembered what to do to keep from getting seasick.

We spent considerable time on the top deck getting acquainted with the ship's captain and some of his officers. He became quite friendly and invited us to his station about 7:00 a. m. the next day to hear some music he was picking up on the radio. Clyde and I were there bright and early. As we listened to the radio we heard *Don't Fence Me In*, sung by Gene Autry. That good country singing was right down our alley. We also heard other music, but Gene Autry's singing always stuck in our memory.

We did not want to hear Frank Sinatra because most GIs thought he made all the girls swoon while they were gone. In fact, they didn't want to see and hear him on U.S.O. tours the servicemen had been going to. Clyde and I were always in battle and it didn't affect us much, but we had been influenced a little by other's jealousy. Bing Crosby seemed to be the big guy for most GIs.

"The *Queen Elizabeth* got us home a little faster than it took us when we were being shipped overseas. The German submarines were no longer a problem as we crossed the Atlantic.

A monument to our nation's liberty

"On March 19, 1945, just as the sun was sinking into the west, I saw one of the most beautiful sights I have ever seen; *The Statue of Liberty.* She welcomed us home, with her torch lifted high. My, what a sight! Passing by her, we were amazed by the lights on buildings and cars as they flashed their headlights. We had forgotten what a beautifully lighted country we had left behind. For over thirty months we had been in a blackout, with the exception of guns firing and bomb explosions as they lighted foreign skies. Our heads were held high and our hearts were full, to think we may have had a small part in fighting battles for this land and keeping those lights shining for a free 'America'. A peace welled up in our hearts as we realized our nation would not have to fear an enemy bomber from Hitler's regime turning off those lights. We knew the war would shortly come to an end. *Author's note (written on September 10, 2001, prior to the terrorist attack in New York City and Washington D. C.)

"We left the ship, got on a train in New York City and went to Fort Dix, New Jersey. There we were treated with one phone call and a meal of anything we wanted to eat. Clyde made the call and I ordered steak, potatoes, and gravy.

"The next day, we boarded a train and headed for Camp Chaffee, located in Fort Smith, Arkansas. On March 23, 1945 we left

Camp Chaffee on a bus headed for McAlester, Oklahoma, for a forty-five day furlough. We arrived home about 10:00 o'clock at night. Since our parents lived on a farm with no telephone, we called a friend, Hazel Shipley. She drove us to the farm and woke up our parents and two sisters. We had a great family reunion.

"On March 27, 1945, we married those two cute little fillies we courted on Coal Creek Bridge. They never did get over those moonlight walks across the bridge.

"On April 12, 1945, while we were still on furlough, President Franklin D. Roosevelt died of a heart attack. This brought grief to America as we lost our great leader on the eve of Germany's surrender on May 7, 1945. The army gave us a fifteen-day extension on our forty-five day furlough.

"Meanwhile, the army came out with a point system for servicemen. The point system determined whether or not we would be discharged from the service of our country. Upon returning to Camp Chaffee, our points were counted, I had eighty-nine and Clyde had eighty-four. Both of us had received the *Silver Star, The Bronze Star, The Good Conduct Medal,* and *The Presidential Unit Citation.* The difference of five points resulted when I received *The Purple Heart,* with an *Oak Leaf Cluster* for being wounded twice, while Clyde received *The Purple Heart* for being wounded once."

**Medals and Ribbons
Of Claude and Clyde**

An Arkansas newspaper captioned their experience of separation as follows:

Twin Brothers Separated for First Time in Army Career

"The difference of one point meant the first separation in their Army career for twin sergeant brothers who recently reported to Camp Chaffee from overseas for processing in the Reception Station of the War Department Personnel Center.

"When the two men reported to the Reception Station and their points were computed, officers in charge considered it advisable to consult higher authority on whether or not discharge for Clyde would also be possible. However, the War Department ruled that such a precedent could not be established, since thousands of other soldiers had eighty-four points, and that adherence to the established policy must be maintained.

* * *

The brothers accepted the War Department's final decision philosophically, and as Clyde pointed out, "I'm no better than any other fellow who has eighty-four points." Claude continued, "I left Camp Chaffee, Arkansas, with my discharge in hand, to end my army career. I entered the United States Army on January 14, 1943 and was discharged on  June 7, 1945, after serving two years, four months, and twenty-four days.

"I left with a sad lonely feeling even though I was returning to my new bride in McAlester. For the first time in our lives Clyde and I were separated. Our service records had not caught up with us at that time. No one seemed to know what happened to former President Roosevelt's letter, stating we were never to be separated. We have wished, many times, that we would have insisted on claiming control of our famous letter. It was reported to us, when we did try to claim it later, of it being burned along with other servicemen's records in a central office in St. Louis, Missouri."

Clyde was sent to a redistribution station for reassignment at Fort Sam Houston, Texas. Clyde pointed out, "It was okay with me to stay in the Army until my time came for the discharge.

"The twenty-eight days I spent there weren't bad at all. I was given my own private room and mess hall privileges. I ate a good breakfast every morning and upon returning to my room I found my bed made. I was required to make an eleven o'clock roll call each morning to see if I was reassigned. After roll call I was free for the day. By twenty days of that leisure living, I was ready to move on. At roll call, they told several other men and me we were being shipped out to Camp Bowie, Texas.

"After riding a train to Camp Bowie, I was assigned to the 781st Chemical Mortar Battalion. Now, I had never fired a mortar in my life, yet they made me platoon sergeant with the responsibility of teaching the entire platoon to fire mortars. I was in luck. Some of the men who had come with me from Fort Sam Houston were in a mortar company in France. They pitched in and helped me learn the procedures of instruction.

"One morning after breakfast, I wasn't feeling well and decided to go to my barracks and lie down for a while. I didn't realize we were having inspection that day. All of a sudden the door opened and our company commander, platoon lieutenant, and a major came in. I jumped to attention. I could see the captain and lieutenant were a little upset after seeing my jacket hanging on the bedpost. The Major said, 'Sergeant, did you fight with the 36th Division?' "

"Yes, Sir was my reply.

"The major looked at the captain and said, 'this man has done his part in this war, let him sleep.' "

"Finally our service records caught up with us. It was noted that Claude and I had been awarded a second *Bronze Star.* They called me in and told me to report to the parade grounds to parade in front of the 36th Division as I received the *Oak Leaf Cluster* to the *Bronze Star.* My required points for discharge were finally met.

"On September 19, 1945, I was discharged from the service of my country at Camp Chaffee, Arkansas, after serving two years, six months, and nineteen days. I got on a bus and headed for home to be reunited with Claude, my new wife, and the other family members."

The Stokes Twins were discharged with five battle stars for fighting in five campaigns of World War II. They served on two continents, Africa and Europe, and in the countries of Italy, France, Germany, and Belgium.

Claude said, "We had seen all the world we wanted to see. We were ready to get back to the greatest land on earth, the good old United States of America."

-8-

Post World War II – Civilian Life

Claude and Clyde went off to fight for their country in World War II as young 'harum-scarum' boys and came home as men. Men who had been tested, tried, and proven to be among the best of loyal Americans willing to lay down their lives for freedom of all people.

Their entry into civilian life came naturally to each of them as they fulfilled their responsibility to provide materially for their new brides and later a family. The first obstacle they encountered was housing. For a short time, they both lived on the farm with their parents, due to the lack of apartments and other places to rent. Defense workers had taken all the available housing at that time.

Claude and Clyde's father faithfully deposited their checks into their accounts while they were in service. Claude's assets included; seven hundred dollars in the bank, eleven white faced and jersey cows, and one-half interest in a 1929 Model A Ford, which he shared with Clyde.

Claude started trying to locate a farm to buy, thereby fulfilling our needs for living quarters

Clyde and Claude

and trying to increase his herd of cattle. He eventually rented a farm located one mile from his famous Coal Creek Bridge where we lived for two years.

Claude was the first one to seek employment as a result of Clyde remaining in the army until he reached the required number of eighty-five points for discharge.

Shortly after Claude's discharge, LaVern, their sister who worked at the Naval Ammunition Depot said, "Claude, why don't you go to work with me? Veterans have the first preference to get a job, and I'm sure you could go right to work." Claude took her suggestion and sought employment at the Naval Ammunition Depot, located on the outskirts of McAlester.

Claude continues his memoirs, "From June 7, 1945 to June 14, 1945, I was unemployed. The Bible says when you take a bride you should not work for one year, but stay home and cheer up your new bride. I suppose I erred on that issue.

"I made application, requesting a position driving heavy equipment, but none was available. I was advised to hire in as a general helper in the 'Five Inch Line' and when a heavy equipment operator position became available, I could be transferred. I took their advice and felt relieved to have a job.

"I started my career on June 15, 1945. Only one week was lost on my Civil Service time as I continued to work for Uncle Sam. This time, not shooting ammunition, but making and shipping it to our troops in the Pacific Area of Operations. It seemed strange to be on the production line instead of the firing line; however, it did give me a sense of fulfillment, knowing I might help our nation defeat the Japanese.

(center) **350mm**

"The ammunition was familiar to me, especially the 350mm shells I started handling on my first day. I felt pretty good to know the McAlester Depot had supplied the ammunition Clyde and I fired so many times. I also hoped some of the shells might help my buddies if they went to the Pacific to fight the enemy.

"The first day on the job brought back some memories of the war. I made my way to the cafeteria for lunch. I was standing in line waiting for my food when a fellow walked up to me and said, 'Do you remember me?' I looked him over and could see that he was about my age.

"I finally said. No, I don't believe I know you. Should I?

"He asked, 'Do you remember an infantryman who was pinned down by a German machine gun, in a ditch, during a battle in Germany? You drove your tank up beside me and told me to stay low in the ditch. Your plan was to pull your tank across the ditch over me, drop the escape hatch, and allow me to crawl up from the bottom and get in the tank with you.' "

"I remembered the incident. He said, 'I am that soldier. I'm Dick Owens.' "

"How in the world did you know me? I asked. Dick was quick to say. 'You don't forget a man who saved your life.' Then he confessed, 'I don't know which scared me the most, that German machine gun or you running that tank over me. I even remember your tank's name, The Oklahoma Wildcat.' "

Dick Owens

"Dick Owens and I became good friends, even though we worked in different departments, we occasionally saw each other. My wife and I invited Dick and his wife Joyce Raye into our home at a later date. It so happened my wife knew Joyce Raye quite well as she and her brother, Neil Lakey, were good friends to my wife's brother, Aubrey Epps.

"I began my career working at the Naval Ammunition Depot as a general helper, in the Five Inch Line, drawing the big sum of sixty-nine cents per hour. I felt lucky to find a job so quickly."

Most young couples today may frown on such a low paying job, but that amounted to $110.40 per month, which was more than mustering-out pay of $52.50 per month allowed returning GIs until they became employed. Claude chose working instead of the mustering-out pay. He called it fluffing off time and wasting government money. He has always been a frugal man, but at the same time, felt dignity in earning a living by working for it.

Salaries for returning GIs were adequate; because living conditions were less than today. One could buy a loaf of bread for ten cents. Couples learned to live within their means by raising gardens, canning food, making clothes, and practicing good management.

When Claude started working he had a few adjustments to make. He continued to have a fighting spirit, especially when anyone said, "I hope this war lasts a little longer because I like making the money." Claude took offense to those kinds of remarks. On one occasion he knocked one of his fellow employees against a wall. He also refused to have anyone cursing him for anything he might do.

Claude and Clyde's Mother made a lasting impression on the twins with the lye soap mouth wash. In all the fifty-six years of being in the Stokes family, I have never heard either Claude or Clyde use profanity in any form.

His supervisors used wise judgment as they counseled with him and helped him adjust to civilian life, while still respecting his point of view.

Claude began climbing the ladder to success in his employment because of his honesty, integrity, aptitude in learning about ammunition, hard work, and a sharp mathematical mind.

He received his first promotion as he was transferred to the Inventory Department, where he learned where all ammunition and its components were stored on the base. His ability to remember lot numbers, and amounts of different ammunition stored, eventually led to another promotion and transfer. He was transferred to the Shipping Department where he remained until his retirement.

Shipping Department
Claude

Mr. Faye Doyle was his new supervisor and was told that Claude was a very good worker, but he would not take a cursing from anyone. He took Claude aside and said, "Stokes, I understand you are an excellent employee and I would like to get along with you."

Claude answered, "Mr. Doyle, I will give you eight hours work for eight hours pay. I will correct any mistakes if you will tell me, but don't ever cuss me out." Mr. Doyle kept his word and so did

Claude. The two men became the best of friends. Years later, Claude became a pallbearer for both Mr. Doyle and his wife even though they were not members of Claude's church, neither did they live in McAlester.

When Mr. Doyle retired, R. H. McKaskle became General Foreman over the Shipping Department. Claude continued to excel in his knowledge of ammunition as he attended classes at Tinker Field, located in Oklahoma City. However, his greatest asset was his actual working experience at the Ammunition Depot. He was awarded, through the recommendation of R. H. McKaskle, the first 'Sustained Superior Performance Award' given at the depot. His award covered the dates of July 1954 to July 1956. He received another like award in 1967. These awards had a cash value attached.

Upon R. H. McKaskle's retirement, Claude was advanced to General Foreman of the Shipping Department. He became known as *The Roadrunner*, as he raced across the depot in his pick-up to check his men. He had two famous statements he used quite often, "I expect eight hours work for eight hours pay, and Man I've got to go, I've got work to do." An artist, Mr. David Franks, depicted Claude in a humorous cartoon.

Claude said, "I hired in at the depot as a general helper for sixty nine cents per hour, and retired with thirty-eight years of Civil Service. I retired, not from The Naval Ammunition Depot, but The Army Ammunition Plant as

Man I've got to go, I've got work to do!

Claude the Roadrunner

General Forman over the Shipping Department. I was privileged to supervise the packaging, crating, and shipping of all ammunition from twenty-two caliber shells to two thousand-pound bombs. We shipped to every training camp in the United States, over-seas troops in the Cuban Crises, Vietnam, Korea, and many other trouble spots in the world.

"I retired on December 21, 1979. I considered it an honor to have served my country. I might add, my salary did make a substantial increase from sixty-nine cents per hour."

35 Years of Federal Service

Colonel Parker and Claude

When Clyde returned to McAlester after his additional three months of service, he found Claude already working at his new employment.

Clyde considered going to work at the McAlester Depot, but his interest was in driving heavy equipment. Since Claude had requested a similar position and had not been successful, Clyde decided to go to work for the McAlester City Bus Lines, which serviced McAlester and many surrounding towns in southeastern Oklahoma. Defense workers were still commuting by bus into McAlester as they continued working at the Naval Ammunition Depot.

Clyde started as a bus driver,

Clyde and City bus.

wearing a uniform and eventually became manager of the company. Finally, automobiles became plentiful, taking away the need for bus runs in this small area; resulting in closing the business, after he worked there for almost nine years.

Clyde continued to have an interest in heavy equipment leading him to find employment in highway construction. His ability to operate motor graders, caterpillars, and other heavy equipment won him recognition over the state. His talent was laying a roadbed to perfection, for the final application of asphalt as he helped construct new highways and repair old ones. Many lovers of beauty travel over the beautiful Talimena Scenic Drive, as it winds through the Ouachita Mountains, located in southeastern Oklahoma, where Clyde did some of his best work.

Clyde and equipment

Clyde began his road construction in 1955 and continued until 1964. He worked for several construction companies including, Anderson, Curry, and Cozad. He enjoyed working outside in the open air and became well known for his skills. However, many dangerous mishaps occurred, which is not unfamiliar to that profession. On one occasion, three hundred and fifty-degree asphalt was dumped on Clyde as he was working. He said, "I can tell you that black, hot, sticky mess was hard to get off. Not to mention the pain from the red, hot mixture. I wasn't too eager to get close to those guys again.

"The most serious accident occurred near Smithville, Oklahoma, when I was pouring gas into a carburetor, when the driver of the equipment stepped on the starter, blowing gas into my face and causing extensive burns to my upper body. I spent eight days in the hospital and was off work for over a month." Clyde escaped death again.

When the Vietnam War was in progress, Clyde decided to apply for employment at the Naval Ammunition Depot, in 1967. He was given the position of driving heavy equipment in the Roads and Grounds Department. During those years of employment, Clyde was presented a 'Sustained Superior Performance Award', for outstanding work by the Public Works Department. Clyde retired in 1985, after working for eighteen and one-half years.

In 1945, both Clyde and Claude scanned Oklahoma, trying to find a farm to buy. Claude was never successful, but Clyde did eventually buy a farm in the Rock Creek area, near Scipio, Oklahoma. He did not live on the farm, but his parents lived there for a period of three years. His sister Eupal and her husband Edward Kerns, also lived there for two years.

Clyde eventually sold the farm when he went into business with Woodrow W. Perrin, a former pastor, as they bought a Christian Bookstore in Sherman, Texas.

The Stokes twins were blessed with three daughters. On March 7, 1947, Karen Eileen was born into Clyde's family. Claude had two daughters, Kay Lynn, born on August 29, 1946, and Lana Lorene, born on March 5, 1957.

Claude and Clyde continued to keep up with news of the 36th Division. They went to their first reunion held at Ft. Hood, Texas. They accompanied two other men from McAlester, Woodrow King and Salty Parker. Claude remembers this first reunion quite well. He said, "Salty was a major in the 36th Division during World War I and told us we didn't have to get a reservation for a room because he could tell them who he was and he would get a room. We didn't get a room and the four of us had to sleep in the car all night. The next day all four of us looked a site, but that disappointment was quickly forgotten.

"We enjoyed getting to see many of our old buddies, especially Audie Murphy, who was the most decorated soldier in World War II. We asked him about his movie experiences and if he was as quick on the draw as the movies portrayed. Audie replied. 'Sure, they have to slow down the cameras to shoot the pictures.' "

"We also enjoyed talking to our former Col. Charles Wilber who had promised us that he was going to make us movie stars after the war when he returned to Hollywood, California. He related an incident with a twinkle in his eye, 'I remember talking with General Dahlquist, when an unknown source of shelling was falling on the enemy. He wanted to know where the shelling was coming from. I told him I didn't know but I knew those . . . Okies were doing it.'"

I recalled the incident. We were pulling the Oklahoma Wildcat in and out of a shed as we were firing shots. We learned a few tricks the Germans had been using.

Through the years, Claude and Clyde have been asked many times, to speak before groups concerning their experience in World War II. One question they were asked tells the story of their success in life. "Were you a Christian when you were fighting in World War II?" Both men answered that question quite well as they spoke to honor veterans at Baptist Men's Breakfast, on November 4, 2001, in The First Baptist Church.

Claude said. "About this time each year, we are invited to speak to history classes in schools in this area and, on occasion, to adult groups. The students ask. 'When you went into battle, were you scared?' "

" I answered the question with a true statement from one of our Generals, when he was asked if American soldiers were scared when they fought battles. He answered, 'Yes, 90% were scared and the other 10% were lying.' "

"The question adults frequently asked, 'Did the war change your life?' I answered their question with yes; it did change my life even more as I became older. There were many small things I had taken for granted all my life. Things like turning on a light when it grew dark, going to the refrigerator when hungry, changing clothes when wet, or getting by a warm fire when it grew cold. I learned to appreciate those small conveniences of life when I served in battle, because there were many wet, cold, hungry, and miserable days. Now I think of those simple things of life and thank God for His blessings.

"I wasn't a Christian while I was in the service and knew very little about God's Word. When I arrived home I was married and started a family. I began going to church, accepted Christ as my personal Saviour and my life was changed forever.

"That change did not come about without some real battles within myself. I made my decision to follow Jesus Christ sound simple, but that was not an easy decision for me to make. I didn't tell them how many times my wife and baby left for church crying and begging me to go with them. I told her I lived a better life than half the church members of Hillcrest Baptist Church didn't drink or smoke, paid my bills, and took good care of my family.

"I thought I was a good guy. That is, until the pastor, Reverend V. O. Baldwin started visiting me. I told him the same thing I had told my wife concerning my morals. He said, 'I agree with you, but that has nothing to do with whether you go to Heaven or Hell. 'You don't have to answer for them or they for you, but you do have to answer to God for your sins. 'God gave His only Son to die on a cross for your sins, and on the third day he arose from the grave. He said, 'All have sinned and come short of the glory of God' "

"Reverend Baldwin explained to me that the only way to Heaven was through *God's Son, Jesus Christ*. My going to Heaven did not depend on how good or bad I was, but it was my decision to accept Jesus Christ as my Lord and Saviors. He read a good bit of the

Bible to me to prove his point. I promised I would attend the revival meeting in progress after a few days.

"While I was at work the next day, those Bible verses were still ringing in my ears, as two other men and I were checking a magazine of ammunition. I was alone in the rear of the magazine and heard a voice, loud and clear, saying, 'This is my beloved Son, in whom I am well pleased.' I looked around and found there wasn't anyone in the magazine but me. I wasn't too smart but I was smart enough to know that God had spoken those words.

"I could hardly wait to attend the revival services at the Hillcrest Baptist Church that evening. On that night in 1947, as the invitation was given, I walked quickly down the aisle of the church and asked Jesus to forgive me of my sins and come into my heart, as my Saviour and Lord. He did, and I told Reverend Baldwin that God wasn't getting much but I would serve Him the rest of my life.

"Later, as I read my Bible, I found the words God spoke to me that day in Matthew 3:17. I finally learned to surrender myself to the greatest leader of all battles; *The Lord God.*

"As I finished my speech on Veteran's Day, I related to them how I had come to realize how many of the incidents in this book can be paralleled to the scripture. I recalled the 'dud shell' not exploding, as we were battling across the Repedo River.

"I had taken credit for being a 'top dog' sergeant, making wise decisions; therefore saving my life and lives of others. The decision was not made by me, but by God. When I read the *Holy Scripture* in *James 5:15-16*, concerning the prayer of faith…'The effectual, fervent prayer of the righteous man (or woman) availeth much.' I knew I was not the 'top man'. God was and is!

"When I returned home, my mom said she never closed her eyes at night or opened them in the mornings that she did not pray for God to return her three boys, Carl, Clyde, and myself home safely. The prayers of my mom plus others brought Clyde and me home safely. Carl returned

Clyde, Claude and Carl

also, after losing only one finger.

"God had a plan for all three of us. He had work to do, through us, and that is the reason we survived World War II."

Claude was ordained as a deacon in the Hillcrest Baptist Church, McAlester, in 1950.He began teaching the Bible to teen-age boys. Throughout the years he taught a men's Bible Class. He has taught the same men for over thirty-six years. He has thirty-five men enrolled in his class and has the best attendance and giving record of any class in the Sunday school of the First Baptist Church in McAlester. Perhaps it is because of a contest for high attendance the church promoted several years ago. Claude came up with the idea of calling his class an army company, with himself as the captain. Any member who was absent had to report to him to be excused, or his name would be put on a blackboard as A.W.O.L. He also threatened them with K. P. duty. All in fun, but it continues to work.

A World War II veteran and retired teacher, Harold Worthen, in his class remarked, "I have never seen anyone who could murder the King's English, and get away with it, like Claude Stokes, but he is the best Bible teacher and scholar I have ever heard."

Claude became a Christian two or three years before Clyde made his decision. Clyde confided that he watched Claude's life to see if he really was standing up for Christian principles during that time of waiting. Clyde said in the Veteran's Day speech, "Claude and I were never separated during World War II or in our lives at that time. That worried me, as I began thinking, Claude was going to Heaven and I was going to Hell. It took a letter from President Franklin D. Roosevelt to keep us together during World War II, but it took God's Son, and my surrender to keep us together for eternity. I did not want to be left behind."

Claude and Clyde are devout members of The First Baptist Church, where they have served in various positions over the past forty years. For twenty-five years they ministered to the elderly in

Colonial Lodge, Claude and Clyde

nursing homes, every week, as they presented God's message and encouragement.

Both Clyde and Claude were always frugal men as they watched their money and managed it wisely. Each of them continued to tithe their income to the Lord. They have never missed giving in that manner through all these years. Each one stated, "I have never been able to out-give the Lord." They each own a three-bedroom brick home, drive two automobiles alike, and do not owe anyone. God has blessed them in a marvelous way, both

Clyde, home and Claude   spiritually, and materially.

They continue to accept invitations to speak in public schools as they share how God has blessed their lives through their experiences in World War II.

Claude was thrilled to receive letters from the students. One little girl said, "Thanks for showing us your medals. I don't care if I am a girl, when I grow up I want to be in the army."

A young boy wrote, "Thank you for telling us about World War II. I liked the part about the people who felt on the back of your neck and they could tell if you were an American."

Claude continued to work after retirement, as he ministered to widows who needed painting or carpentry work done. He did

Will Rogers School, Claude and Clyde

this work at a minimum charge. He believed the widows were being overcharged. He took on his servant-role for the Lord, while Clyde used his giving to the needs of the unfortunate in a different way.

They have always honored their Father and Mother, as Claude bought a house next door for them in their latter years, where Jess was happy to raise a huge vegetable garden. During their last months of life, professional care became a necessity. The twins visited their parents every day as long as they lived. Jess lived to be ninety-four, and Nancy lived to be one hundred-one.

On November 17, 2001, Claude made the statement, "One of God's commandments says, *'Honor thy Father and Mother, that thy days may be long on the earth.'* I suppose we've done okay, because we are seventy-eight years old today. God only promised us seventy."

EPILOGUE

Claude's final remarks: "As we reach the end of our memoirs, and especially, our experiences with The 636th Tank Destroyer Battalion, in World War II, we wish to make some apologies.

"It would have been impossible to name all the tank crews within the battalion. We were a fighting unit, bonded together, to help and support each other. The officers and men of the battalion from Colonel Charles Wilburn, our commander, to the private who loaded our guns will always be special to us.

"I am so sorry I cannot remember the names of all the men who served on the crew of the Oklahoma Wildcat. Some only served a few days or a few weeks. Some men did not serve long enough for an acquaintance to be established, but they all served well. After fifty-seven years since World War II, my old memory is not what it used to be.

"We sincerely regret not writing our adventures earlier in life so that all our old buddies could have read it. May those who remain find enjoyment, comfort, and inspiration in reading personal accounts of our lives, through our youth, World War II, and in our twilight years?

"Clyde and I count it a privilege and blessing to have served our beloved country. We challenge and pray for our future generations to stand courageously for our country, our homes, and our God."

* * *

Author's comments: Many miracles of inspiration have taken place in our writing. Surely it's no coincidence that the account of Claude's returning to the United States and viewing *The Statue of Liberty* found in Chapter 8, was recorded on September 10, 2001. It was an overwhelming moment when this author wrote the account, feeling the passion that these two men had for our nation. A great spiritual awakening of God's purpose in my life, love for family, and allegiance to our nation engulfed me. This one miracle of God's leadership has inspired me to continue writing inspirational writings to our great nation.

Another miracle took place involving the story of *The Lost Battalion* found in Chapter 5. Having studied World War II history and writing about the Stokes twins has caused my senses to be on alert to connected news items. On October 17, 2001, the Army National Guard troops from Texas were deployed to help protect the McAlester Army Ammunition Plant and to the lesser extent, the city of McAlester.

It is a miracle that The 141st Infantry of the 36th Division would be deployed to McAlester to protect the very plant where Claude and Clyde spent most of their lifetime working. This 141st Infantry Division was *The Lost Battalion* that Claude, Clyde, and the Oklahoma Wildcat helped rescue during World War II, fifty-seven years ago. The favor has now been returned. [1]

Caught up in the poignant accounts of World War II History, and the first-hand accounts of their participation in numerous battles, with miraculous escapes from death, related by Claude and Clyde, has been a blessing to me. Perhaps, you too, may have experienced an awakening to your call for greater appreciation of many unsung heroes who died to keep faith alive and to help preserve our nation's freedom. *GOD BLESS AMERICA.*

God Bless America Banner, First
Baptist Church. 1999. Designed and
directed construction by Madlyn
Stokes. Assisted by: Lorene Auston,
Wilma Adams, Jaunita Maisano,
Barbara McPherson, Ann Everly,
Dovie Sartin, Claude Stokes, and
Billie Stipe.

The Cross-, artist Georgia Pace, Wilburton, Oklahoma

ENDNOTES

Introduction: Pages 1-6

    l.   Dick Swoboda, "Stokes Twins Known Jolly Well; But Who's Horne?", McAlester
      News-Capital, Associated Press, January 23, l977, p. l.

Chapter 1: Early Years of the Stokes Twins, Pages 7-24.

    1. "World War 1 and 11", The World Book Encyclopedia, 11th ed., 1953, Vol. 18, p. 8870.
    2. "Franklin Delano Roosevelt", The World Book Encyclopedia, 11th ed., l958, Vol. 14, p. 7022.
    3. Clifton Daniel e. g. John W. Kirshon et al., "Allies Are Evacuated From Dunkirk", Chronicles of the 20th Century, (Darling Kindersly Publishing, Inc.), 2nd ed., 1995, p. 509.

Chapter 2: World War II Training, Pages 25-36.

    1. "Franklin Delano Roosevelt", The World Book Encyclopedia, 11th ed., 1958, Vol., 14, p. 7029.

Chapter 3: World War II-Africa, Pages 37-48.

1. Betty Debham, "A History of Africa", <u>Universal Press Syndicate</u>, (The Mini Page Publishing Co., Inc.), McAlester News-Capital, February 13, 2001.
2. Carl C. Granmer, "Nazi Dreams of Conquest Are Brought To Bloody Conclusion", <u>Associated Press</u>, Oklahoma City Times, p. 2, col. 3.
3. Ibid., p 2, col. 3.
4. "The North African Front", <u>The World Book Encyclopedia</u>, 1958 ed, p. 8886.
5. Clifton Daniel e. g. John W. Kirshon, et al., "Allied Forces Land in North Africa", <u>Chronicles of the 20th Century</u>, (Darling Kindersly Publishing, Inc.), 2nd ed., 1995, p. 543.
6. "Sahara Desert", <u>The World Book Encyclopedia</u>, 1958 ed., Vol. 15, p. 7136.
7. Richard A. Huff, ed., "Texans Were Mobilized At Camp Bowie", <u>The Pictorial History of the 36th "Texas" Infantry Division</u>, (Published by The 36th Division Association, Austin, Texas), p. 2.
8. Tom Sherman, <u>Seek, Strike, Destroy</u>, "The History of the 636 Tank Destroyer Battalion", 1986, ed., p. 15.

Chapter 4: World War II-Invasion of Italy, Pages 49-86.

1. Sherman, <u>Seek, Strike, Destroy</u>, p. 16.
2. Clifton Daniel e.g. John W. Kirshon, et al., "Allies Land in Sicily, Capture Palermo", <u>Chronicles of the 20th Century</u>, (Darling Kindersly Publishing, Inc.), 2nd, 1995, p. 552.
3. Huff, <u>Fighting 36th</u>, "Salerno".
4. Dave Turner, <u>Tank Destroyer Forces, WWW II</u>, "Salerno", (Turner Publishing Company), 1991, p. 46.
5. Sherman, <u>Seek, Strike, Destroy</u>, pp. 223-225.
6. Ibid. p. 28.
7. Huff, <u>The Fighting 36th</u>, "Million Dollar Mountain".
8. Sherman, <u>Seek, Strike, Destroy</u>, p. 55.

9. John A. Hyman, ed., 36th Division in World War II, "Montecassino Bombed",(Texas Military Forces Museum-Austin, Texas.), 1998, pictorial history.

10. Huff, The Fighting 36th, Montecassino Bombed".

11. Ibid.

12. Ibid. "Japanese-Americans".

13. Sherman, Seek, Strike, Destroy, p.71

14. Ibid. 80

15. Ibid. 87

16. Huff, The Fighting 36th, "The Southern France Invasion".

17. Huff, The Fighting 36th, "Italy Summary".

18. Huff, The Fighting 36th, "Cavalcade".

Chapter 5: World War II-Invasion of Southern France, Pages 87-108.

1. Richard A. Huff, ed., "The Invasion of Southern France", The Pictorial History of the 36th "Texas Infantry Division, (Published by The 36th Division Association, Austin, Texas).

2. Ibid., "Convoy Sails".

3. Ibid., "Grave Decision".

4. Ibid., "Paratroopers Contacted".

5. Ibid., "On To Grenoble".

6. Tom Sherman, Seek, Strike, Destroy, "August, 1944", pp.97, 98.

Chapter 6: World War II-Invasion of Germany, Pages 109-130

1. Tom Sherman, Seek, Strike, Destroy, "December, 1944", p. 149.

2. Ibid., p. 153.

3. Ibid., p. 160.

4. Tom Sherman, Seek, Strike, Destroy, "Outnumbered Armored Devils Blast Seven Enemy Tanks", pp. 163, 164.

5. Carl C. Granmer, "Nazi Dreams of Conquest Are Brought To Bloody Conclusion", <u>Associated Press</u>, Oklahoma City Times, May 7, 1945, p. l.

6. Richard A. Huff, ed., <u>The Pictorial History of the 36th "Texas" Infantry Division,</u> (Published by the 36th Division Association, Austin, Texas). p. 3.

Chapter 8: Post World War II-Civilian Life, Pages 137-149.

1. James Beaty, ed., "Texas National Guard unit keeping watch at McAAP", <u>McAlester</u> <u>News-Capital & Democrat</u>, p. 20, November 11, 2001.

BIBLIOGRAPHY

A collection of books on World War II in our home library have been indispensable in the course of our research, most of which give coverage in chronological order of the conflict in Europe.

We highly recommend all the books listed to those who appreciate reading about some of the valiant men who sacrificed so much to save the world from tyranny in World War II.

Richard A. Huff, ed., <u>Pictorial History of the 36th "Texas" Infantry Division</u>, (Published by The 36th Division Association), Austin, Texas.

Tom Sherman, <u>Seek, Strike, Destroy</u>, "The History of the 636 Tank Destroyer Battalion",
     1986.

Dave Turner, ed., <u>Tank Destroyer Forces- World War II</u>, (Turner Publishing Company),
     1991.

John A. Hyman, ed., <u>The 36th Division in World War II</u>, Texas Military Forces-Austin,
     Texas), Pictorial History, 1998.

Clifton Daniel e.g. John W. Kirshon, et al., <u>Chronicles of the 20th Century</u>, (Darling
     Kindersly Publishing, Inc.) , 2nd ed., 1995.

GLOSSARY

Americano: Italian word for American.

Anzio Annie: Name given to a German 170mm railroad gun.

Axis Sally: German radio antagonist.

Bully beef: (British ration), dried strips of beef.

D Bar: An invasion chocolate candy bar (equivalent to a full day food supply).

Dear John Letter: Notification of termination of a relationship.

Five-in-one: (enough for five), pork-beans, bacon, Spam, crackers, and coffee.

Fritzy Boy: Nickname given to a German.

Hard Tack: British biscuit.

Kraut: American nickname given to German.

Hiya: Indian name for cow manure.

K Ration: crackers, cheese, beef bullion for soup, dehydrated eggs, and coffee.

LCI: Landing craft for infantry.

LST: Landing ship for tanks.

Mama Mia: Italian words for good gracious.

Nein: German word for no.

Tedesco: Italian word for German.

24771620R00095

Made in the USA
Charleston, SC
04 December 2013